Marvin D. Bisbee

Songs of the Pilgrims

Marvin D. Bisbee

Songs of the Pilgrims

ISBN/EAN: 9783337266004

Printed in Europe, USA, Canada, Australia, Japan

Cover: Foto ©Thomas Meinert / pixelio.de

More available books at **www.hansebooks.com**

SONGS OF THE PILGRIMS.

WITH AN INTRODUCTION BY

REV. H. M. DEXTER, D.D.

They shook the depths of the desert's gloom
With their hymns of lofty cheer.

EDITED BY M. D. BISBEE.

BOSTON AND CHICAGO:

Congregational Sunday-School and Publishing Society.

PREFACE.

My Dear Mr. Bisbee: —

You ask me to preface, by a few words, your
collection of Pilgrim verses. I am glad you have
gathered them together, and I hope you will
publish them. Some of them may be no great
things looked at simply as fruits of the Muse,
but they are all wholesome and well meant.
Without exception, they have a good, strong,
healthy savor, — like opening a drawer where
thyme and other aromatics have been drying;
and some of them have the rhythm of sweet
music in them. Taken together, they are
eminently worthy of preservation, as the most
distinctively New England, of any collection
of odes, songs, ballads, or whatever, which
could be made. They all deserve kindly
remembrance and a good place in our history,
as some of them do in our poetry.

With sincere affection,

Faithfully yours,

HENRY MARTYN DEXTER.

CONTENTS.

vi   *Contents.*

Contents.

ARRIVAL AT CAPE COD.

WILLIAM BRADFORD'S ACCOUNT.

BEING thus arrived in a good harbor and brought safe to land, they fell upon their knees & blessed ye God of heaven, who had brought them over ye vast & furious ocean, and delivered them from ye periles & miseries thereof, againe to set their feete on ye firme & stable earth, their proper elemente. And no marvell if they were thus joyefull, seeing wise Seneca was so affected with sailing a few miles on ye coast of his owne Italy; as he affirmed, that he had rather remaine twentie years on his way by land, than pass by sea to any place in a short time; so tedious & dreadfull was ye same unto him.

But hear I can not but stay and make a pause and stand half amased at this poore peoples presente condition; and so I thinke will the reader too, when he well considers ye same. Being thus passed ye vast ocean, and a sea of troubles before in their preparation (as may be remembered by yt which wente before), they had now no friends to wellcome them, nor inns to entertaine or refresh their weatherbeaten bodys, no houses, or much less townes to repaire too, to seeke for succoure. It is recorded in Scripture as a mercie to ye apostle & his shipwrecked company, yt the barbarians shewed them no smale kindnes in refreshing them, but those savage barbarians, when they mette with them (as after will appeare) were readier to fill their sides full of arrows than otherwise. And for ye season, it was winter, and they that know ye winters of yt countrie know them to be sharp & violent & subject to cruel & fierce storms, deangerous to travill to known places, but much more to serch an unknown coast. Besids, what could they see but a hidious & desolate wildernes full of wild beasts & wild men? and what multituds ther might be of them they knew not. Neither could they, as it were, goe up to ye tope of Pisgah, to vew from this wildernes a more goodly cuntrie to feed their hops; for which way soever they turned their eys (save upward to ye heavens) they could have little solace or content in respecte to any outward objects. For sumer being done, all things stand upon them with a weatherbeaten face; and ye whole cuntrie, full of woods & thickets, represented a wild & savage view. If they looked behind them, ther was ye mighty ocean which they had passed, and was now as maine barr and goulfe to separate them from all ye civill parts of ye world. If it be said they had a ship to succoure them, it is trew, but what heard they daly from ye Mr & company? but yt with Speade they should looke out a place with their shallop, wher they would be at some neare distance, for ye season was shuch, as he would not stirr from thence till a safe harbor was discovered by them wher they would, and he might goe without danger; and that victells consumed apace, but he must & would keep sufficient for them selves & their returne. Yea, it was muttered by some that if they gott not a place in time, they would turne them & and their goods ashore & leave them.

Let it also be considred what weake hopes of supply & succoure they left behind them yt might bear up their minds in this sade condition and trialls they were under; and they could not but be very smale. It is true indeed, indeed ye affections & love of their brethren at Leyden was cordiall & entire towards them, but they had little power to help them, or them selves; and how ye case stode betweene them & ye marchants at their coming away, hath already been declared. What could now sustaine them but ye spirite of God & his grace? May not and ought not the children of those fathers rightly say: *Our faithers were Englishmen which came over this great ocean, and were ready to perish in this wilderness, but they cried unto ye Lord, and he heard their voyce and looked on their adversitee.*

SONGS OF THE PILGRIMS.

THAT GRAY, COLD CHRISTMAS DAY.

December 25, 1620.

THEY sailed away from Provincetown Bay
   In the fireless light of the sun,
And they came at night to a havened height,
   And the journey at last was done.
With rain and sleet were the tall masts iced,
   And frosty and dark was the air,
But they looked from the crystal sails to Christ
   As they moored in the harbor fair.
      The sky was cold and gray,
         And there were no ancient bells to ring,
         No priests to chant, no choirs to sing,
         No chapel of baron, lord, or king,
        That gray, cold winter day.

The snow came down on the vacant seas
   And deep on the lone rocks lay ;

But their axes rung 'mid the evergreen-trees,
And followed the Sabbath day.
The Christmas came, in a crimson haze,
And the workmen said at dawn :
" Shall our axes swing on this day of days
When the Lord of Light was born ? "
The sky was cold and gray,
And there were no ancient bells to ring,
No priests to chant, no choirs to sing,
No chapel of baron, lord, or king,
That gray, cold Christmas day.

"The old towns' bells we seem to hear,
They are ringing sweet on the Dee :
They are ringing sweet on the Haerlem Meer,
And sweet on the Zuyder Zee.
The pines are frosted with snow and sleet :
Shall we our axes wield,
When the bells of Lincoln are ringing sweet
And the bells of Austerfield ? "
The sky was cold and gray,
And there were no ancient bells to ring,
No priests to chant, no choirs to sing,
No chapel of baron, lord, or king,
That gray, cold Christmas day.

Then the master said : " Your axes wield ;
　Remember ye Malabarre Bay,
And the covenant there with the Lord ye sealed ;
　Let your axes ring to-day.
You may talk of the old towns' bells to-night,
　When your work for the Lord is done ;
And your boats return, and the shallops light
　Shall follow the light of the sun.
　　　　The sky is cold and gray,
　　　　　And here are no ancient bells to ring,
　　　　　No priests to chant, no choirs to sing,
　　　　　No chapel of baron, lord, or king,
　　　　　This gray, cold Christmas day.

" If the Lord was born on Christmas day,
　And the day of him is blest,
Then low at his feet the evergreens lay,
　And cradle his Church in the West.
Immanuel waits at the temple gates
　Of the nation to-day ye found,
And the Lord delights in no empty rites —
　To-day let your axes sound ! "　　　　　．
　　　　The sky was cold and gray,
　　　　　And there were no ancient bells to ring,
　　　　　No priests to chant, no choirs to sing,

No chapel of baron, lord, or king,
   That gray, cold Christmas day.

Their axes rung through the evergreen-trees,
   Like the bells on the Thames and Tay,
And they cheering sang by the windy seas,
   And they thought of Malabarre Bay.
On the lonely heights of Burial Hill
   The old Precisioners sleep,
But did ever men with a nobler will
   A goodlier Christmas keep —
      When sky was cold and gray,
         And there were no ancient bells to ring,
         No priests to chant, no choirs to sing,
         No chapel of baron, lord, or king,
            That gray, cold Christmas day?
                     — *Hezekiah Butterworth.*

ROBINSON OF LEYDEN.

HE sleeps not here; in hope and prayer
   His wandering flock had gone before,
But he, the shepherd, might not share
   Their sorrows on the wintry shore.

Before the Speedwell's anchor swung,
  Ere yet the Mayflower's sail was spread,
While round his feet the Pilgrims clung,
  The pastor spake, and thus he said :

" Men, brethren, sisters, children dear,
  God calls you hence from over sea ;
Ye may not build by Haerlem Meer,
  Nor yet along the Zuyder Zee.

Ye go to bear the saving word
  To tribes unnamed and shores untrod ;
Heed well the lessons ye have heard
  From those old teachers taught of God.

Yet think not unto them was lent
  All light for all the coming days,
And heaven's eternal wisdom spent
  In making straight the ancient ways.

The living fountain overflows
  For every flock, for every lamb.
Nor heeds, though angry creeds oppose
  With Luther's dike or Calvin's dam."

He spake ; with lingering, long embrace,
  With tears of love and partings fond,

They floated down the creeping Maas,
  Along the Isle of Ysselmond.

They passed the frowning towers of Briel,
  The " Hook of Holland's " shelf of sand,
And grated soon with lifting keel
  The sullen shores of fatherland.

No home for these !   Too well they knew
  The mitred king behind the throne ;
The sails were set, the pennons flew,
  And westward ho ! for worlds unknown.

And these were they who gave us birth,
  The Pilgrims of the sunset wave,
Who won for us this virgin earth,
  And freedom with the soil they gave.

The pastor slumbers by the Rhine, —
  In alien earth the exiles lie, —
Their nameless graves our holiest shrine,
  His words our noblest battle-cry !

Still cry them, and the world shall hear,
  Ye dwellers by the storm-swept sea !
Ye have not built by Haerlem Meer,
  Nor on the land-locked Zuyder Zee !
                              — *O. W. Holmes.*

THE EMBARKATION.

THE band of Pilgrim exiles in tearful silence
 stood,
While thus outspake, in parting, John Robinson
 the good :
" Fare thee well, my brave Miles Standish !
 Thou hast a trusty sword ;
But not with carnal weapons shalt thou glorify
 the Lord.
Fare thee well, good Elder Brewster !　Thou art
 a man of prayer ;
Commend the flock I give thee to the Holy Shep-
 herd's care.
And thou, beloved Carver ! — what shall I say
 to thee ?
I need, in this my sorrow, that thou shouldst
 comfort me.
In the furnace of affliction must all be sharply
 tried ;
But nought prevails against us, if the Lord be
 on our side.
Farewell, farewell, my people !　Go, and stay
 not the hand,

But precious seed of freedom sow ye broadcast
    through the land.
Ye may scatter it in sorrow, and water it with
    tears,
But rejoice for those who gather the fruit in
    after years ;
Ay! rejoice that ye may leave them an altar
    unto God,
On the holy soil of freedom, where no tyrant's
    foot hath trod.
All honor to our sovereign, his majesty King
    James,
But the King of kings above us the highest
    homage claims."
Upon the deck together they knelt them down
    and prayed, —
The husband and the father, the matron and the
    maid ;
The broad blue heavens above them, bright with
    the summer's glow,
And the wide, wide waste of waters, with its
    treacherous waves below ;
Around, the loved and cherished, whom they
    should see no more,
And the dark, uncertain future stretching dimly
    on before.

Oh, well might Edward Winslow look sadly on
his bride!

Oh, well might fair Rose Standish press to her
chieftain's side!

For with crucified affections they bowed the
knee in prayer,

And besought that God would aid them to suffer
and to bear;

To bear the cross of sorrow — a broader shield
of love

Than the royal cross of England, that proudly
waved above.

The balmy winds of summer swept o'er the glittering seas;

It brought the sign of parting, — the white sails
met the breeze;

One farewell gush of sorrow, one prayerful
blessing more,

And the bark that bore the exiles glided slowly
from the shore.

Thus they left that goodly city, o'er stormy seas
to roam,

But they knew that they were pilgrims, and this
world was not their home.

There is a God in heaven, whose purpose none
    may tell;
There is a God in heaven who doeth all things
    well.
And thus an infant nation was cradled on the
    deep,
While hosts of holy angels were set to guard its
    sleep;
No seer, no priest or prophet, read its horoscope
    at birth,
No bard in solemn Saga sung its destiny to
    earth;
But slowly, slowly, slowly as the acorn from the
    sod,
It grew in strength and grandeur, and spread its
    arms abroad.
The eyes of distant nations turned toward that
    goodly tree,
And they saw how fair and pleasant were the
    fruits of liberty!
Like earth's convulsive motion before the earth-
    quake's shock,
Like the foaming of the ocean around old Ply-
    mouth Rock,
So the deathless love of freedom, of the majesty
    of right,

In all kindred and all nations, is rising in its
  might ;
And words of solemn warning come from the
  honored dead, —
Woe, woe to the oppressor if righteous blood be
  shed !
Rush not blindly on the future ! Heed the lessons of the past !
For the feeble and the faithful are the conquer-
  ors at last.

— *Lizzie Doten.*

FOREFATHERS' DAY.

THE memory of the faithful dead
  Be on their children's hearts this day !
Your fathers' God, their hosts that led,
  Will shield you through the stormy way.

Your Saviour bids you seek and save
  The trampled and the oppressed of earth ;
At his command the storm to brave,
  Faithful and true, come boldly forth !

Their suffering though your souls must share,
　Though pride oppress and hate condemn,
Stand up ! and breathe your fearless prayer
　For those in bonds as bound with them !

Unheeded falls the fierce command
　That bids the struggling soul be dumb !
Shout with a voice to rouse a land !
　Bid the free martyr spirit come !

Searcher of hearts, to thee we bow, —
　Uphold us with thy staff and rod ;
Our fervent hearts are ready now, —
　We come to do thy will, O God !
　　　　　　　　— *M. W. Chapman.*

THE LIBERTY SONG.[1]

Tune : *Hearts of Oak.*

COME, join hand and hand, brave Americans
　all,
And rouse your bold hearts at fair Liberty's call ;
No tyrannous acts shall suppress your just claim,
Or stain with dishonor America's name.

[1] Sung at the *first* celebration of the landing at Plymouth, 1769.

CHORUS.

In freedom we're born, and in freedom we'll
  live;
      Our purses are ready,
      Steady, friends, steady,
Not as slaves, but as freemen, our money we'll
  give.

Our worthy *Forefathers* — let's give 'em a
  cheer! —
To climates unknown did courageously steer;
Through oceans to deserts for freedom they
  came,
And dying, bequeathed us their freedom and
  fame.

Their generous bosoms all danger despised,
So highly, so wisely, their birthright they prized;
We'll keep what they gave — we will piously keep,
Nor frustrate their toils on the land or the deep.

The Tree their own hands had to liberty reared,
They lived to behold growing strong and revered;
With transport they cried: "Now our wishes we
  gain,
For our children shall gather the fruits of our
  pain."

How sweet are the labors that freemen endure,
That they shall enjoy all the profits secure.
No more such sweet labors Americans know,
If Britons shall reap what Americans sow.

Swarms of placemen and pensioners soon will
    appear,
Like locusts deforming the charms of the year;
Suns vainly will rise, showers vainly descend,
If we are to drudge for what others shall spend.

Then join hand in hand, brave Americans all;
By uniting we stand, by dividing we fall;
In so righteous a cause let us hope to succeed,
For heaven approves of each generous deed.

All ages shall speak with amaze and applause
Of the courage we'll show in support of our
    laws;
To die we can bear, but to serve we disdain;
For shame is to freemen more dreadful than pain.

This bumper I crown for our Sovereign's health,
And this for Britannia's glory and wealth;
That wealth and that glory immortal may be,
If she is but *just*, and we are but *free*.

      — Hon. John Dickinson, Delaware, and
        Dr. Arthur Lee, Virginia.

THE MAYFLOWER.

HOW dar'st thou try this stormy path,
    Thou frail and struggling bark !
Old England's shores are shut from sight
    Amid the gathering dark.
The friends who waved their sad adieu
    Have homeward gone to weep,
And thou art left, a lonely waif,
    Upon the boundless deep.

Night closes round thy little group
    Of aching, homesick hearts,
That strive to hide the thoughts which rise,
    And quench the tear that starts ;
But hard it is, on wings of faith,
    To mount o'er present fears,
And see the glory that may break
    Around the distant years.

Yet sail thou on, thou shalt not fail
    To reach yon waiting shores ;
Thou carriest treasures costlier far
    Than Ophir's golden stores ;

If Cæsar's bark must needs be safe
  Amid the angry waves,
The men thou bearest can not sink
  In ocean's gloomy caves.

Sail gladly on, the world behind
  Is rent with hate and strife ;
The canker of a thousand years
  Is feeding on its life ;
Yea, welcome, as thy truest friend,
  This broad, dividing sea ;
Its stormy ramparts are thy shield,
  The world beyond is free.

The little seed, by Pilgrim hands
  In fear and weakness sown,
May wait through long and weary years
  Before to fullness grown ;
But it shall stand, a mighty tree,
  In glory and in pride,
And through the rising ages stretch
  Its fruitful branches wide.

Then sail thou on, though torn and tossed,
  By tempests driven and hurled,

Thou hast the charter which shall shape
  And rule a coming world.
The tyrant kings, with haughty power,
  Who scorned thy low estate,
Shall roam as exiles in the earth,
  And on thy bidding wait.

Fair freedom from this hour shall date
  A new and wondrous birth ;
The light of liberty shall rise
  To spread o'er all the earth ;
The monarch's gilded throne shall grow
  A cheap and childish thing,
For man in dignity shall stand,
  And God alone be king.

Earth's ancient tribes and lands remote ;
  Where Indus rolls his tides,
Or where the Northern dwellers climb
  The snowy mountain sides ;
Where the fierce Arab spurs his steed
  Across the burning plain,
Or fur-clad Russians drive the deer
  With freely flowing rein ;

Where the dark Ethiop spreads his tent
  On Afric's Eastern shores ;
Or forest hunters skim the waves
  With lightly dipping oars. —
All lands beneath the circling sun,
  All islands of the sea,
As centuries roll. shall taste the fruit
  From this fair Pilgrim tree.
                — *Increase N. Tarbox.*

PLYMOUTH AND THE BAY.

THEY tell of the mighty founders,
  And the empires great of old,
Of the rough gigantic Nimrod,
  And of Romulus the bold,
Of the fierce barbaric warriors,
  And the pirates of the flood,
Who built their thrones by plunder,
  And stained their courts with blood ;
But we sing, in a grander story,
  Of the men who crossed the sea
To change these western forests
  To an empire of the free ;

The hand of the Lord was with them,
  Along their perilous way,
And they laid their firm foundations
  At Plymouth and the Bay.

They would not bend the conscience
  To suit a tyrant's frown,
And at the feet of haughty kings
  They would not bow them down ;
They met their proud oppressors
  With calm, undaunted eye,
As men long used to suffer,
  And not afraid to die ;
In the strength of God they trusted,
  In the love of God they wrought ;
Nor gold, nor earthly glory,
  Nor praise of men, they sought.
In humble faith and patience
  They lived their little day,
And laid their strong foundations
  At Plymouth and the Bay.
              — *Increase N. Tarbox.*

THE PILGRIMS.

HOW slow yon tiny vessel plows the main !
Amid the heaving billows now she seems
A toiling atom.   Then from wave to wave
Leaps madly, by the tempest lashed, or reels,
Half-wrecked, through gulfs profound.

Moons wax and wane,
But still that lonely traveler treads the deep.
I see an ice-bound coast, towards which she
steers
With such a tardy movement that it seems
Stern winter's hand hath turned her keel to
stone,
And sealed his victory on her slippery shrouds.
They land ! they land !   Not like the Genoese,
With glittering sword, and gaudy train, and eye
Kindling with golden fancies.   Forth they come
From their long prison, — hardy forms, that
brave
The world's unkindness, — men of hoary hair,
And virgins of firm heart, and matrons grave,
Who hush the wailing infant with a glance.
Bleak nature's desolation wraps them round, —

Eternal forests, and unyielding earth,
And savage men, who through the thickets peer
With vengeful arrow. What could lure their
    steps
To this drear desert? Ask him who left
His father's home to roam through Haran's
    wilds,
Distrusting not the guide who called him forth,
Nor doubting, though a stranger, that his seed.
Should be as ocean's sands.

                  But yon lone bark
Hath spread her parting sail.

                  They crowd the strand,
Those few lone Pilgrims. Can ye scan the woe
That wrings their bosoms, as the last frail link
Binding to man and habitable earth
Is severed? Can ye tell what pangs were there,
What keen regrets, what sickness of the heart,
What yearnings o'er their forfeit land of birth,
Their distant dear ones?

                  Long with straining eye
They watch the lessening speck. Heard ye no
    shriek

Of anguish when that bitter loneliness
Sank down into their bosoms?   No! They turn
Back to their dreary famished huts, and pray! —
Pray, — and the ills that haunt this transient life
Fade into air.   Up in each girded breast
There sprang a rooted and mysterious strength,
A loftiness, to face a world in arms,
To strip the pomp from scepters, and to lay
Upon the sacred altar the warm blood
Of slain affections when they rise between
The soul and God.

            And can ye deem it strange
That from their planting such a branch should
    bloom
As nations envy?   Would a germ, embalmed
With prayer's pure teardrops, strike no deeper
    root
Than that which mad ambition's hand doth strew
Upon the winds, to reap the winds again?
Hid by its veil of waters from the hand
Of greedy Europe, their bold vine spread forth
In giant strength.

              Its early clusters, crushed
In England's wine-press, gave the tyrant host

A draught of deadly wine.   Oh! ye who boast
In your free veins the blood of sires like these,
Lose   not   their   lineaments.   Should   mammon
    cling
Too close around your heart, or wealth beget
That bloated luxury which eats the core
From manly virtue, or the tempting world
Make faint the Christian purpose in your soul,
Turn ye to Plymouth's Beach, and on that rock
Kneel in their footprints, and renew the vow
They breathed to God.

—Mrs. L. H. Sigourney.

HYMN.

SONS of the noble sires
    Who braved proud ocean's waves
        For freedom's sake !
Say, will ye quench those fires
Their faith and love inspires,
And, standing on their graves,
        Their paths forsake?

Shall freedom find a grave
On this blood-ransomed soil?
 Must we be slaves?
Our fleeting lives to save,
Must we no mercy crave,
But with the bondman toil,
 Branded as knaves?

Shall despots here bear sway —
The iron scepter here display,
 Our lips to close?
Sons of the Pilgrims! Say,
Will ye these lords obey,
And ask them when you may
 The truth disclose?

No, no! we answer, No!
The truth we'll fearless show
 While breath remains;
Did not our Saviour so?
Would he the truth forego?
Or shrink when bade the foe,
 T' escape from pains?

While then a slave is found,
While man by man is bound,
 We'll speak and pray;

We 'll wear the bondman's chains,
We 'll bear the bondman's pains,
We 'll hear when he complains, —
    We 'll do and say.
                    — *George Russell.*

CLARK'S ISLAND.

HAIL! hallowed spot, where freedom's rays
    First darted o'er the wanderer's ways,
        And gave him rest;
First brought the dawn of brighter days, —
        Thy shores are blest!

But dark the clouds that lingered round
The island which the Pilgrim found
        In time long gone,
And deep and drear the thrilling sound
        Of gathering storm.

Aye, dark indeed, whose night of yore
That rocked the Mayflower near the shore
        On wintry tides, —
For dark the waves that round thee roar,
        And wash thy sides.

But bright the star that lent its ray
To bear the traveler on his way
      From childhood's seat;
That lighted up so fair a day
      For his retreat.

Oh, who would ask a holier bed
Than where he laid his weary head,
      And nobly slept?
For though the Pilgrim long hath fled,
      His spirit's left.

Then, hail the spot where first the sound
Of freedom shook the sacred ground
      In early days,
And filled the hills and forests round
      With gladsome praise!
            — *Hersey B. Goodwin.*

THE PILGRIM FATHERS.

A VOICE of grief and anger,
    Of pity mixed with scorn,
Moans o'er the waters of the West,
    Through fire and darkness borne;

And fiercer voices join it, —
  A wild, triumphant yell !
For England's foes, on ocean slain,
  Have heard it where they fell.

What is the voice that cometh
  Athwart the spectered sea ?
The voice of men who left their homes
  To make their children free ;
Of men whose hearts were torches
  For freedom's quenchless fire ;
Of men whose mothers have brought forth
  The sire of Franklin's sire.

They speak ! the Pilgrim Fathers
  Speak to you from their graves !
For earth hath muttered to their bones
  That we are soulless slaves !
The Bradfords, Carvers, Winslows,
  Have heard the worm complain,
That less than men oppress the men
  Whose sires were Pym and Vane !

What saith the voice that boometh
  Athwart the upbraiding waves ?
Though slaves are ye, our sons are free ;
  Then why will you be slaves ?

The children of your fathers
  Were Hampden, Pym, and Vane!
Land of the sires of Washington,
  Bring forth such men again!
— *Ebenezer Elliot, the Corn-law Rhymer of*
England.

FOREFATHERS' DAY.

O'ER the white surges of the sea
    A wave-worn ship comes sailing on,
Carrying aloft, all visibly,
    The marks of many a tempest gone.

Without a pilot at the helm,
    On this far-past memorial day,
Fearless of what may overwhelm,
    She steers within the unknown bay.

Beneath the bold and rocky steep
    That guards that lone and wintry shore,
She casts her anchor to the deep,
    Her long and stormy voyage o'er.

I see stern manhood, bold and strong,
    Girt as for any rugged task,

Striding the slippery deck along,
   Nor caring in the sun to bask.

And, side by side with manhood's pace,
   Under that bleak and frowning sky,
I see fair woman's gentle face,
   Braving the air as fearlessly.

The memory of their distant home,
   So dear to every filial heart,
Still throbs beneath their spirits' dome,
   Telling how hard from it to part.

And as they gaze upon the land,
   Into the depths of forests old,
No pleasant views their souls command,
   But only scenes all dark and cold.

There are no spires of cities fair,
   No monuments of wealth and taste
That lift their winning beauty there,
   And bid them to such welcome haste.

O'er vale and hill the pathless wood
   Stretches its scepter far away ;
Its shadows all the landscape brood,
   And dim the light of brightest day.

In such a scene, what heritage
  These lonely voyagers to cheer?
What prizes that their choice engage
  Amid these barren wilds appear?

Have they the conqueror's thirst for blood?
  And would they win a warrior's fame?
And here, beyond this Western flood,
  Carve with the sword a soldier's name?

Nay; they have come across the sea
  From the dear land that gave them birth,
To worship God in liberty
  In these remotest ends of earth.

Ah! on the crest of Plymouth Rock
  They built more grandly than they knew,
And to that sacred stone there flock
  Unnumbered Pilgrims, brave and true.

Are we the sons of Pilgrim sires?
  Where'er we roam, o'er land and sea,
Burn in our hearts the living fires
  That prove such high nativity?

Prize we the memory of the day
  That brought our fathers o'er the deep?

And would we, fearlessly as they,
A Pilgrim's faith unfaltering keep?

Do we forsake a life of ease?
Do we reject the rule of sense?
And, seeking not ourselves to please,
Choose rather to be exiled hence?

When we are tempted to provide
The good that earthly passions crave —
Ambition, luxury, and pride —
Flee we across the distant wave?

The scepter of this lower world,
Held o'er our heads to bid us bow,
Let us, with canvas wide unfurled,
O'er some Atlantic turn our prow!

By self-denial's sacrifice,
And self-devotion to the right,
To heaven's guidance lift our eyes,
And from all evil take our flight!

So may we prove the hallowed tie
That binds us to that Pilgrim band,
And live again, all filially,
Their life, so holy, pure, and grand!
— *A. L. Stone.*

SONG.[1]

Tune: *British Hero.*

A LL hail the day that ushers in
　　The period of revolving time,
In which our sires, of glorious fame,
Bravely through toils and dangers came,

Novanglia's wilds to civilize,
And wild disorder harmonize,
To plant Britannia's arts and arms,
Plenty, peace, freedom — pleasing charms,

Derived from British rights and laws,
That justly merit our applause ;
Darlings of heaven, heroes brave,
You still shall live, though in the grave.

Live, live, within each grateful breast,
With reverence for your names possessed ;
Your praises on our tongues shall dwell,
And sires to sons your actions tell.

To distant poles their praise resound,
Let virtue be with glory crowned.

[1]Sung at the *second* celebration, 1770.

Ye dreary wilds, each rock and cave,
Echo the virtues of the brave.

They nobly braved their indigence,
Death, famine, sword, and pestilence.
Each toil, each danger they endured,
Till for their sons they had procured

A fertile soil, profusely blest
With nature's stores, and now possessed
By sons who gratefully revere
Our fathers' names and memories dear.

Plymouth, the great mausoleum,
Famous for our forefathers' tomb;
Join, join the chorus, one and all,
Resound their deeds in Colony Hall!
— *Alexander Scammel.*

REMEMBER, Lord, thy folk whom thou
To wilderness hast brought;
Let not thine own inheritance
Be sold away for nought.
— *Anne Bradstreet.*

HYMN.

[1770.]

TO thee the tuneful anthem soars,
  To thee, our fathers' God, and ours ;
This wilderness we chose our seat ;
To rights secured by equal laws,
From persecution's iron claws,
  We here have sought our calm retreat.

See ! how the flocks of Jesus rise !
See ! how the face of Paradise
  Blooms through the thickets of the wild !
Here Liberty erects her throne ;
Here Plenty pours her treasures down ;
  Peace smiles, as heavenly cherubs mild.

Lord ! guard thy favors ; Lord ! extend
Where farther western suns descend ;
  Nor southern seas the blessings bound ;
Till Freedom lift her cheerful head,
Till pure Religion onward spread,
  And, beaming, wrap the globe around.
                                    — *Mather Byles.*

MONDAY, 11–21, DECEMBER, 1620.

MORNING was breaking over Gurnet Head;
   Up sprang Miles Standish from his hem-
      lock bed,
With cold and anxious forethought hard be-
   stead.

The chilling shadows of the shortest day
Delayed the brightness of the dawning ray,
While round the smoldering fire his comrades
   lay.

He raked the embers with a branch of fir,
Threw o'er the coals pine-knots and juniper,
And watched the fragrant, crackling blazes stir.

The merry sound, suggesting better cheer
Of warmth, and light, and comfort waiting near,
One and another waked, intent to hear.

A tall and slender form, with winsome face —
Its fine lines beaming with benignant grace —
And aspect gentler than became the place,

Stood at his side — to whom then Standish said:
" I fear me, governor, lest this rough work, bred
Of wave and winter, shall leave many dead.

" Haste is upon us.   Somewhere in this bay
It groweth urgent that we fix, this day,
Some spot where we may build and make a way."

" Even so," replied the governor ; " yet my faith
Is strong that, as the ancient Psalmist saith,
' Who cry for help, them He delivereth.'

" While ' on the Sabbath day we rested ' here,
Giving the hours, as well, to humble prayer,
Doubt fled, and to my soul all things grew clear,

As, to the eye of faith, that cloudy sign
Which Israel followed as its guide benign,
Rested, for us, upon that dark shore line."

John Carver pointed, as he spake, away
Whither, three miles or more across the bay,
The gleam from sunrise on a hillside lay.

Spake out then Master Coppin, standing near :
" An' 't please your worships, shallow gulfs, as
       here,
Have this one law : ' Hard by the channel steer.'

" Two days of ebb and flood to my close quest
Have marked, without mistake, one course as
       best ;
The tide-flow inward maketh south-south-west.

" And though yon slopes across these nearer
   shoals
Invite the coming of sea-weary souls,
Not that way is it that deep water rolls."

" 'T is well," the governor said.   " Break first
   our fast ;
With prayer let speed be made ; put sail to mast ;
Answer approacheth for our problem vast."

Uncovering round the sturdy watch-fire's blaze,
He next, accordant to their pious ways,
Led them to heaven in speech of prayer and
   praise.

Then turned they, hungry, to their simple
   cheer, —
As in the fatherlands that sent them there, —
Thankful for biscuit, cheese, and bitter beer.

In haste they bounded o'er the shallop's side,
Pushed off with ease upon the rising tide,
And to their sail the help of oars supplied.

They caught the north-west wind off Saquish
   sand,
And soon the young flood lent its powerful hand
To tug their keel toward the long-wished-for
   strand.

By Long Beach Head eastward the channel
    veered,
And for a mile scarcely the mainland neared,
While straight before the favoring breeze they
    steered.

That land gave greeting in the young day's light,
Well-wooded and well-hilled, and clean and
    bright;
A home-like look it had — a pleasant sight!

Cleared ground on one side offered homesteads
    good,
While close around it, as grim sentinels, stood
Some lofty monarchs of primeval wood.

Sharp to the west the tide-way sudden strayed
Toward where a bowlder on its side was laid.
Near by an entering stream its music made.

" Let us debark," impetuous Standish bade ;
To whom the governor bowed his willing head,
And for the bowlder's side the boat was sped.

Shoreward, in sand the rock lay bedded steep,
Seaward, it bordered upon waters deep ;
Easy the eager crew could on it leap.

Landed, they rambled through those forest
  nooks,
Heard something like the "caw" of their own
  rooks,
Found cornfields here and there, and running
  brooks ;

Oaks, pines, beech, walnut, cedar, birch, and
  ash —
As goodly trees as the Old Country has —
With plum, asp, cherry, vines, and sassafras ;

Sorrel and yarrow, brooklime, liverwort,
"Great stores of leekes and onyons," many a
  sort
Of wild herb, good for use of health, or hurt.

"A spit's depth of black earth" indorsed the
  mold ;
While, that all Indian "signs" were plainly old,
Freedom of entry to new-comers told.

And now the brief day stands at its high noon.
Spake Carver : "Goodmen ! darkness hasteth
  soon,
With small help for us from the waning moon.

" These shores beseem ' for scituation good ' ;
Here maize, and fowl, and fish plan plenteous
       food,
And desolation offereth quietude.

" What harbor for our shipping it can prove,
To test and settle doth us next behoove ;
So to our soundings let us instant move."

As down the bluffs they haste, bound in one
       thrall,
For a brief moment, on a hillock tall,
As by a common impulse, lingered all.

The scene was winsome, — calm the waters lay,
And soft the sweet light stretching far away, —
A summer picture for a winter's day.

Quoth Bradford : " If to us God blessing gave,
Who should die serving here, should comfort
       have,
Nor miss man's benison on his lowly grave."

" Ay !" answered Carver. " Ay ! better sleep
       here " —
His word awaiting proof that self-same year —
" Than in the Rhine-washed aisles of St. Pierre."

The shallop's heavy head was sent about,
And, with their fathom-line and plummet stout,
That 't was a harbor fair, put out of doubt.

Then toward Clark's Island back their course
they lay,
The night in bivouac there once more to stay,
And hie them to their ship the following day.

They had the work in hand done to their best,
Yet dreamed not, as that sun went down the
west,
That to the ages they had made bequest!

—H. M. Dexter.

FROM " THE PRESENT CRISIS." [1]

COUNT me o'er earth's chosen heroes, — they
were souls that stood alone,
While the men they agonized for hurled the
contumelious stone ;
Stood serene, and down the future saw the
golden beam incline

[1] By permission of Houghton, Mifflin & Co.

To the side of perfect justice, mastered by their
    faith divine,
By one man's plain truth to manhood and to
    manhood's great design.

For humanity sweeps onward ; where to-day the
    martyr stands,
On the morrow crouches Judas with the silver in
    his hands ;
Far in front the cross stands ready and the
    crackling fagots burn,
While the hooting mob of yesterday in silent
    awe return
To glean up the scattered ashes into history's
    golden urn.

'T is as easy to be heroes as to sit the idle slaves
Of a legendary virtue carved upon our fathers'
    graves ;
Worshipers of the light ancestral make the pres-
    ent light a crime ; —
Was the Mayflower launched by cowards, steered
    by men behind their time ?
Turn those tracks toward past or future that
    make Plymouth Rock sublime ?

                  —*James Russell Lowell.*

ODE.

NOT all the loftiest memories
　　That rose on earlier days,
When, with the trump and sacrifice,
　　And swelling pomp of praise,
Men gathered to their pillared halls,
　　'Mid garlands, joy, and wine,
To gaze on heroes round the walls,
　　In marble made divine,

And pour the deep libation there
　　To victors passed away;
On minds whose wonders, rich and rare,
　　Poured splendor on their day, —
Not all in finer hearts can vie
　　With those that summon here
To lift, on freedom's clarion high,
　　The anthem of our cheer!

We sing a nobler race than passed
　　In ancient times to glory;
We sing of deeds that shall outlast,
　　In fame, all classic story;

Of men who fought for God, and gave
    Home for a desert shore, —
With hearts too panoplied and brave
    To quail beneath its roar!

Of exiles of a deathless line
    And proud, unshrinking brow;
Lone pilgrims to a rocky shrine,
    Where a people bend them now;
A rocky shrine, unsheltered, rude,
    Where the wild wolf from his lair
Shrieked through the pathless solitude,
    And broke the voice of prayer!

We sing of heroes who outdid
    The boast of chivalry;
Whose valor braved the shock amid
    A stormy sea and sky;
Whose deeds were deeds of mercy, done
    To persecuted man;
Whose wreaths were wreaths of triumph, won
    In virtue's fearless van!

New England's fathers! Men who dared
    The agony of years;
Whom pale oppression never spared,
    But could not bow to tears;

Who, 'mid the howl of winter, fled,
And your banner here unfurled,
And conscience in her pride outled
Unfettered to the world.

Pilgrims of glory! There shall rise
Fast praise from heart and tongue
Of all for whom in sacrifice,
Like martyr-saints, ye sprung;
And their children's children shall outpour
From echoing clime to clime,
New pæans for the toils ye bore
In a nation's morning-time.

Two hundred years their cloudy wings
Expand above your graves;
And lo, what wide-flashed glory flings
O'er all New England's waves!
Fathers of liberty! To ye
We lift the wine-cup now;
Yours be the hallowed memory
That consecrates our vow!

And should the voice of prophecy
That's doomed us to the dust
E'er chant the requiem of the free,
By tyranny accursed,

Oh, be a remnant true to her !
　　Sons whom New England bore,
Together seek one sepulcher
　　On Plymouth's sounding shore !
　　　　　　　— *Grenville Mellen.*

HYMN.[1]

THE brittle bark is on the gale,
　　Heaven guides her course and swells the
　sail ;
The Pilgrims reach yon welcome shore,
All vocal with the songs they pour.

Keen round them blows the winter's air ;
The weary wanderers kneel for prayer ;
From opening clouds a voice is given ;
Pilgrims, there 's nothing true but heaven !

What though no mystic cloud, nor flame,
Led on the wanderers as they came?
By faith they saw the one true God
Was guardian of the way they trod.

[1] Written for December 22, 1831.

God of our fathers, hear our prayer!
This church be still and long thy care;
And, grateful at this day's return,
Fresh incense at thy shrine shall burn.

How long shall erring mortals feel
The exclusive, the unholy zeal
The golden gates of heaven to close
On all they dare to call thy foes?

These doors we open fling, and free
To all, Great God, who call on thee;
If warm their hearts in Christian deeds,
Who shall exclude them for their creeds?

Here may they drink from living springs
The light and life the gospel brings;
And, healed by Siloa's waters, deem
Thy power and bounty fed the stream.

Rise! Bethlehem's star, and spread thy blaze
To every land in cheering rays,
Till angels, in the glad employ,
Cast down their crowns and shout for joy!

— *Anonymous.*

ODE FOR THE 22D OF DECEMBER.[1]

Tune: *America.*

SONS of renowned sires !
 Join in harmonious choirs,
 Swell your loud songs ;
Daughters of peerless dames !
Come with your mild acclaims,
Let their revered names
 Dwell on your tongues !

From frowning Albion's seat,
See the famed band retreat,
 On ocean tost ;
Blue tumbling billows roar,
By keel scarce plowed before,
And bear them to this shore,
 Fettered with frost.

By yon wave-beaten Rock,
See the illustrious flock
 Collected stand ;

[1] Composed for the Anniversary Festival at Plymouth in 1792.

To seek some sheltering grove,
Their faithful partners move,
Dear pledges of their love
  In either hand.

Not winter's sullen face,
Not the fierce tawny race
  In arms arrayed;
Not hunger shook their faith,
Not sickness' baleful breath,
Nor Carver's early death,
  Their souls dismayed.

Watered by heavenly dew
The germ of empire grew,
  Freedom its root.
From the cold Northern pine,
Far toward the burning line,
Spreads the luxuriant vine,
  Bending with fruit.

Columbia! child of heaven!
The best of blessings given
  Rest on thy head;
Beneath thy peaceful skies,
While prosperous tides arise,
Here turn thy grateful eyes,
  Revere the dead.

Afterward revised to: —

[Columbia! child of heaven!
The best of blessings given
  Be thine to greet;
Hailing this votive day,
Looking with fond survey
Upon the weary way
  Of Pilgrim feet.]

Here trace the moss-grown stones,
Where rest their moldering bones,
  Again to rise;
And let thy sons be led
To emulate the dead,
While o'er their tombs they tread
  With moistened eyes.

Sons of renowned sires!
Join in harmonious choirs,
  Swell your loud songs;
Daughters of peerless dames!
Come with thy mild acclaims,
Let their revered names
  Dwell on your tongues.
                    — *John Davis.*

HYMN FOR THE 22D OF DECEMBER.[1]

Tune: *Ferry.*

WHEN o'er the billows heaving deep,
    The fathers of our race,
The precepts of their God to keep,
    Sought here their resting-place,

That gracious God their path prepared,
    Preserved from every harm,
And still for their protection bared
    His everlasting arm.

His breath, inspiring every gale,
    Impels them o'er the main,
His guardian angel spreads the sail,
    And tempests howl in vain.

For them old ocean's rocks are smoothed;
    December's face grows mild;
To vernal airs her blasts are soothed,
    And all their rage beguiled.

When Famine rolls her haggard eyes
    His ever-bounteous hand
Abundance from the sea supplies,
    And treasure from the sand.

[1] Sung at the Forefathers' celebration of 1803.

Nor yet his tender mercies cease ;
His over-ruling plan
Inclines to gentleness and peace
The heart of savage man.

And can our stony bosoms be
To all these wonders blind ?
Nor swell with thankfulness to thee,
O Parent of mankind ?

All-gracious God ! inflame our zeal ;
Dispense one blessing more —
Grant us thy boundless love to feel,
Thy goodness to adore.

— *John Quincy Adams.*

FROM " THE PRESENT CRISIS." [1]

THEY were men of present valor, stalwart
  old iconoclasts,
Unconvinced by axe or gibbet that all virtue was
  the past's ;
But we make their truth our falsehood, thinking
  that hath made us free,

[1] By permission of Houghton, Mifflin & Co.

Hoarding it in moldy parchments, while our tender spirits flee
The rude grasp of that great impulse which drove them across the sea.

They have rights who dare maintain them ; we are traitors to our sires,
Smothering in their holy ashes freedom's new-lit altar-fires ;
Shall we make their creed our jailer? shall we in our haste to slay,
From the tombs of the old prophets steal the funeral lamps away
To light up the martyr-fagots round the prophets of to-day?

New occasions teach new duties ; time makes ancient good uncouth ;
They must upward still, and onward, who would keep abreast of truth ;
Lo ! before us gleam her camp-fires ! we ourselves must pilgrims be,
Launch our Mayflower, and steer boldly through the desperate winter sea,
Nor attempt the future's portal with the past's blood-rusted key.

—*James Russell Lowell.*

HYMN FOR THE 22D OF DECEMBER.

(1799.)

Tune: *Old Hundred.*

HAIL! Pilgrim Fathers of our race,
    With grateful hearts your toils we trace;
Again this votive day returns,
And finds us bending o'er your urns.

Jehovah's arm prepared the road:
The heathen vanished at his nod;
He gave his vine a lasting root;
He loads its goodly boughs with fruit.

The hills are covered with its shade;
Its thousand shoots like cedar spread;
Its branches to the sea expand,
And reach to broad Superior's strand.

Of peace and truth the gladsome ray
Smiles in our skies and cheers the day;
And a new empire's splendent wheels
Roll o'er the top of Western hills.

Hail! Pilgrim Fathers of our race,
With grateful hearts your toils we trace;
Oft as this votive day returns,
We 'll pay due honors to your urns.

AN ODE.

(1806.)

Ask thy Father, and he will shew thee. — *Moses.*
The Lord hath done great things for us. — *Psalmist.*

W̅ITH sympathetic sway,
  Commemorate the day
 Our fathers came ;
From England's hostile shore,
By persecution sore,
Crimsoned with martyrs' gore
 They crossed the main.

An asylum to seek,
They crossed the raging deep,
 Conscience their star ;
By God's approving grace,
It aids them to this place
In this drear wilderness.
 God's name revere.

By troubles drove from home,
Amid stern winter's gloom,
 They landed here ;

[1] In commemoration of the landing of our Forefathers in Ply.
mouth, December 22, 1620.

No friend to give relief,
Or mitigate their grief,
But foes to mercy deaf,
    With bow and spear.

They foes nor dangers fear,
Nor winter's cold severe,
    Nor death's cold hand,
That thinned them off apace,
Nor godly Carver's death,
All could not shake their faith,
    To quit the land.

Then while we tread the soil,
The blessings of their toil,
    We'll not forget
The end for which they came:
To spread the gospel's fame;
While we enjoy the same,
    God's praise repeat.

Sons of Columbia, join
To praise the hand divine;
    Daughters rejoice;
And as ye praise his name,
Sing our Forefathers' fame,
Who hither laid your claim.
    Loud raise your voice.

Though yonder silent tombs
Contain their moldering bones,
   Their names yet live ;
The wonders they have done
Shall go from son·to son,
   That people yet unborn
Shall sing his praise.

— *F. B.*

THE PILGRIMS.[1]

MEN in the middle of life, austere and
   grave in deportment,
Only one of them old, the hill that was nearest
   to heaven,
Covered with snow, but erect, the excellent
   elder of Plymouth.
God had sifted three kingdoms to find the wheat
   for this planting,
Then sifted the wheat, as the living seed of a
   nation ;
So say the chronicles old, and such is the faith
   of the people.

— *Longfellow.*

[1] By permission of Houghton, Mifflin & Co.

THE SAINTED SIRES.

WHILE Pilgrim's sons, a festive throng,
    To sainted sires their homage pay,
Be this the burthen, the burthen of their song,
    And rapture animate the lay :

CHORUS.

Hail, ye Pilgrims !
Ye sainted Pilgrims, hail !
Till hours, and years, and time shall fail.

By heroes led, by virtue warmed,
    Conducted by the Almighty hand,
They braved the ocean, the ocean and the storm,
    And freedom sought in unknown land.

The perils of the ocean past,
    Fresh dangers quickly them surround ;
Shrill screams the savage, the savage o'er the
        blast,
    And rocks and hills repeat the sound.

The barbarous foe to battle fly,
    Intent on bloody deeds and spoil ;
Swift flies the arrow, the arrow through the sky,
    But victory crowns the Pilgrim's toil.

Success attend the good and brave,
The meed of praise to them belongs ;
Virtue shall triumph, shall triumph o'er the grave,
And angels join their rapturous songs.
                    Hail, ye Pilgrims !
Ye sainted Pilgrims, hail !
When earth, and sky, and time shall fail.
                              — *Anonymous.*

FROM " INTERVIEW WITH MILES STANDISH."[1]

                    The ghost drew up his chair
And said : " My name is Standish.
I come from Plymouth, deadly bored
    With toasts, and songs, and speeches,
As long and flat as my old sword,
    As threadbare as my breeches ;
They understand us Pilgrims ! They,
    Smooth men with rosy faces,
Strength's knots and gnarls all pared away,
    And varnish in their places !

[1] By permission of Houghton, Mifflin & Co.

We had some toughness in our grain :
  The eye to rightly see us is
Not just the one that lights the brain
  Of drawing-room Tyrtæuses ;
They talk about their Pilgrim blood,
  Their birthright high and holy !
A mountain stream that ends in mud
  Methinks is melancholy.
—James Russell Lowell.

FROM " BIGLOW PAPERS." [1]

      That famous bark,
That brought our sires intrepid,
  Capacious as another ark,
For furniture decrepit ;
For, as that saved of bird and beast
  A pair for propagation,
So has the seed of these increased
  And furnished half the nation.
—James Russell Lowell.

[1] By permission of Houghton, Mifflin & Co.

HYMN.[1]

Tune: *Old Hundred.*

OUR fathers' God! to thee we raise,
　　With one accord, the song of praise;
To thee our grateful tribute pay,
Oft as returns this festal day.

With tearful eyes we here will trace
Thy wonders to the Pilgrim race,
And while those wonders we explore,
Their names extol, thy name adore.

Our fathers' God! thy own decree
Ordained the Pilgrims to be free;
In foreign lands they owned thy care,
And found a safe asylum there.

When the wide main they traversed o'er,
And landed on this sea-beat shore,
The Pilgrims' Rock must e'er proclaim
Thy guardian care was still the same.

Our fathers' God! while here we trace
Our lineage to the Pilgrim race,

---

[1] Sung at Plymouth, 22 December, 1806.

Oh, may we like those Pilgrims live,
And in the sons the sires revive.

Our fathers' God ! to thee we raise,
With one accord, the song of praise ;
To thee our grateful tribute pay,
Oft as returns this festal day.

— *Abiel Holmes.*

———

SONG.[1]

Tune: *Hail Columbia.*

THE Almighty gave the high behest —
    Rise an empire in the West,
  Freedom's loved and last abode,
  Freedom's loved and last abode.
Our fathers bowed to his decree,
And dauntless braved an unknown sea,
    Climbed the foaming precipice,
    Plunged adown the black abyss,
    Where the maddening tempest raves,
    Where meet the sky the mountain waves.

[1] Sung at celebration of 22 December, 1806, New York.

CHORUS.

Sons of freedom, swell the song ;
To sainted sires the notes prolong,
Till the echoing skies around
Sound the trumpet-note rebound.

Lo ! the heaven-protected band
Seeks the forest-fringed strand.
  Roars the rough hybernal blast,
  Roars the rough hybernal blast.
Countless perils wait them here,
Sickness pale and famine drear,
  Pining want and dire disease
  Float in every blasting breeze ;
  Desolation's ghastly form
  Rides in every death-winged storm.

Murderous hordes of savage foes
Round the pious Pilgrims rose,
  With flinty hearts and blood-stained hands,
  With flinty hearts and blood-stained hands.
From horror's haunts, in wilds immense, .
Lo ! the gloomy bands condense.
  Hark ! the war-whoop's frantic yell
  Bursts from yonder dismal dell ;
  Savage forms of demons dire
  Wrap the Pilgrims' camp in fire.

The God at whose behest
Rose an empire in the West,
   Freedom's loved and last abode,
   Freedom's loved and last abode,
Protected still, with mighty hand,
The Pilgrims in a barbarous land.
   Raise the song of festive mirth
   To those who gave an empire birth;
   Their names and memories shall rest
   Enthroned in every freeman's breast.
          — *Thomas Greene Fessenden.*

FROM "BIGLOW PAPERS."[1]

O STRANGE new world, thet yit wast never young!
Whose youth from thee by gripin' need was wrung,
   Brown foundlin' o' the woods, whose baby-bed
Was prowled roun' by the Injun's cracklin' tread,
An' who grew'st strong thru shifts an' wants an' pains,
Nussed by stern men with empires in their brains.
          — *James Russell Lowell.*

[1] By permission of Houghton, Mifflin & Co.

SONG.

(December 22, 1807.)

HAIL! sons of the Pilgrims, assembled to
    pay
Festivity's rite to our fathers in glory!
May the ardor of friendship enliven the lay,
   And their virtues be told while we glow with
     the story.
       With the patriot's fire
       Be inflamed each desire,
To all that is noble each bosom aspire ;
For, long as old earth on her axle shall turn,
On the altars of freemen pure incense should
    burn.

When tyranny bigotry's banners upreared,
   Those fathers, for conscience, for freedom,
    self-banished,
Confiding in heaven, o'er the wild billow steered,
   And in Holland found refuge, while bigotry
    vanished ;
       There, strangers awhile
       From their friends, from their isle,

See them sojourn in hope, in adversity smile ;
Till, raising again the white sail to the wind,
They plow the rough main their own region to
        find.

Long tossing in doubt o'er the 'wildering wave,
    The pilot yet timid to brave the commotion ;
Them hailing to freedom, from perils to save,
    Columbia displayed her blue skirt from the
        ocean.
            In Plymouth they land,
            On the bleak, barren strand,
Yet they 're strong in their shield — an Omnipo-
        tent hand :
For there to their wanderings a period they find,
And their brows with the laurels of freedom first
        bind.

The savage his quiver exhausted in vain ;
    He rose, but his tomahawk idle descended ;
Independent, the Pilgrims moved free o'er the
        plain ;
    Magnanimity nerved them, their bravery
        defended ;
            Though environed by foes,
            They found calm repose,

While the wilderness blossomed and smiled like
    the rose ;
Till late to the grave as they smoothly declined,
To their offspring their virtue, a birthright,
    resigned.

When Albion their heirs to enslave vainly strove,
    When lunatic committed aggression,
They lowered in the combat, the assailants hence
    drove,
    Independence they won, of their rights kept
    possession.
        Then oft will we tell,
        In the feast of the shell,
The deeds of their fame, till with transports we
    swell ;
And teach the sweet infant that smiles on his
    sire
To pant for like fame, and to glow with like fire.

Though society's base were by faction assailed,
    Or the bane of our safety by flattery were
    varnished ;
Though the veteran be seen in his hamlet
    unmailed,

Retired from the council, his laurels
  untarnished ;
    Yet the foe on our coast,
    Lo ! he flies to his post ;
His valor impels, in himself he 's a host ;
And with him the sons of New England shall
  fly,
Resolved to live honored, or nobly to die.

Yes ; now from the East see aggression impend !
  Ye venerable shades, your remembrance shall
    fire us ;
Our rights shall be sacred, our laws we 'll
  defend ;
  Our Union shall strengthen, true glory inspire
    us ;
    If the bolt be but hurled.
    Shall our flags be unfurled :
Though few, yet their fame shall extend o'er the
  world ;
While the honors and laurels that deck our brave
  tars
Shall end but with time, and but fade with the
  stars !

Thus, oft in our pilgrimage, memory shall glow
 As the tale of the past comes with pleasure
  attendant ;
And the boast of our nation latest ages shall
 know —
 Our fathers in glory, their sons independent!
  Then glad be your song,
  Ye convivial throng !
Roll, roll the full chorus of rapture along !
For, long as old earth on her axle shall turn,
On the altars of freemen pure incense must burn.
    — *Joseph Warren Bracket.*

FROM " THE COURTSHIP OF MILES STANDISH." [1]

PRISCILLA.

AS he opened the door, he beheld the form
 of the maiden
Seated beside her wheel, and the carded wool
 like a snow-drift
Piled at her knee, her white hands feeding the
 ravenous spindle,

---

[1] By permission of Houghton, Mifflin & Co.

While with her foot on the treadle she guided
the wheel in its motion.

Open wide on her lap lay the well-worn psalm-
book of Ainsworth,

Printed in Amsterdam, the words and the music
together;

Rough-hewn, angular notes, like stones in the
wall of a churchyard,

Darkened and overhung by the running vine of
the verses.

Such was the book from whose pages she sang
the old Puritan anthem,

She, the Puritan girl, in the solitude of the
forest,

Making the humble house and the modest apparel
of homespun

Beautiful with her beauty, and rich with the
wealth of her being!

.   .   .   .

"I have been thinking all day," said gently
the Puritan maiden,

"Dreaming all night, and thinking all day, of
the hedge-rows of England, —

They are in blossom now, and the country is all
like a garden;

Thinking of lanes and fields, and the song of
the lark and the linnet,
Seeing the village street, and familiar faces of
neighbors
Going about as of old, and stopping to gossip
together,
And, at the end of the street, the village church,
with the ivy
Climbing the old gray tower, and the quiet
graves in the churchyard.
Kind are the people I live with, and dear to me
my religion ;
Still my heart is so sad, that I wish myself back
in old England.
You will say it is wrong, but I can not help it ; I
almost
Wish myself back in old England, I feel so
lonely and wretched."

THE PROPOSAL.

Thereupon answered the youth : " Indeed, I
do not condemn you ;
Stouter hearts than a woman's have quailed in
this terrible winter.
Yours is tender and trusting, and needs a
stronger to lean on ;

So I have come to you now with an offer and
　　proffer of marriage,
Made by a good man and true, Miles Standish,
　　the captain of Plymouth!"

.　　.　　.　　.　　.　　.　　.　　.　　.

But as he warmed and glowed, in his simple and
　　eloquent language,
Quite forgetful of self, and full of the praise of
　　his rival,
Archly the maiden smiled and, with eyes over-
　　running with laughter,
Said, in a tremulous voice, "Why don't you
　　speak for yourself. John?"

THE SAILING OF THE MAYFLOWER.

Out of the sea rose the sun, and the billows
　　rejoiced at his coming;
Beautiful were his feet on the purple tops of the
　　mountains;
Beautiful on the sails of the Mayflower riding at
　　anchor,
Battered and blackened and worn by all the
　　storms of the winter.
Loosely against her masts was hanging and flap-
　　ping her canvas,

Rent by so many gales, and patched by the
hands of the sailors.
Suddenly from her side, as the sun rose over the
ocean,
Darted a puff of smoke and floated seaward;
anon rang
Loud over field and forest the cannon's roar, and
the echoes
Heard and repeated the sound, the signal gun
of departure!
Ah! but with louder echoes replied the hearts of
the people!
Meekly, in voices subdued, the chapter was read
from the Bible;
Meekly the prayer was begun, but ended in fer-
vent entreaty.
Then from their houses in haste came forth the
Pilgrims of Plymouth,
Men and women and children, all hurrying down
to the sea-shore,
Eager, with tearful eyes, to say farewell to the
Mayflower,
Homeward bound o'er the sea, and leaving them
here in the desert.

. . . .

Meanwhile the master, alert, but with dignified
    air and important,
Scanning with watchful eye the tide and the
    wind and the weather,
Walked about on the sands, and the people
    crowded about him
Saying a few last words, and enforcing his care-
    ful remembrance.
Then, taking each by the hand, as if he were
    grasping a tiller,
Into the boat he sprang, and in haste shoved off
    to his vessel,
Glad in his heart to get rid of all this worry and
    flurry,
Glad to be gone from a land of sand and sick-
    ness and sorrow,
Short allowance of victual, and plenty of noth-
    ing but gospel !
Lost in the sound of the oars was the last fare-
    well of the Pilgrims.
O strong hearts and true ! not one went back in
    the Mayflower !
No, not one looked back, who had set his hand
    to the plowing !

Soon were heard on board the shouts and
    songs of the sailors
Heaving the windlass round, and hoisting the
    ponderous anchor.
Then the yards were braced, and all sails set to
    the west wind,
Blowing steady and strong : and the Mayflower
    sailed from the harbor,
Rounded the point of the Gurnet, and leaving
    far to the southward
Island and cape of sand and the field of the first
    encounter,
Took the wind on her quarter, and stood for the
    open Atlantic,
Borne on the send of the sea and the swelling
    hearts of the Pilgrims.

Long in silence they watched the receding sail
    of the vessel,
Much endeared to them all, as something living
    and human ;
Then, as if filled with the Spirit, and wrapt in a
    vision prophetic,
Baring his hoary head, the excellent elder of Ply-
    mouth

Said, " Let us pray ! " and they prayed, and
thanked the Lord and took courage.
Mournfully sobbed the waves at the base of the
rock, and above them
Bowed and whispered the wheat on the hill of
death, and their kindred
Seemed to awake in their graves, and to join in
the prayer that they uttered.
Sun-illumined and white, on the eastern verge of
the ocean,
Gleamed the departing sail like a marble slab in
a graveyard :
Buried beneath it lay forever all hope of
escaping.

THE WOOING.

" Truly, Priscilla," he said, " When I see you
spinning, and spinning,
Never idle a moment, but thrifty and thoughtful
of others,
Suddenly you are transformed, are visibly
changed in a moment ;
You are no longer Priscilla, but Bertha the beautiful spinner."
Here the light foot on the treadle grew swifter
and swifter ; the spindle

Uttered an angry snarl, and the thread snapped
    short in her fingers ;
While the impetuous speaker, not heeding the
    mischief, continued :
" You are the beautiful Bertha, the spinner, the
    Queen of Helvetia ;
She whose story I read at a stall in the streets of
    Southampton,
Who, as she rode on her palfrey o'er valley and
    meadow and mountain,
Ever was spinning her thread from a distaff
    fixed to her saddle.
She was so thrifty and good that her name
    passed into a proverb.
So shall it be with your own, when the spinning-
    wheel shall no longer
Hum in the house of the farmer and fill its
    chambers with music.
Then shall the mothers, reproving, relate how it
    was in their childhood,
Praising the good old times and the days of
    Priscilla the spinner ! "
Straight uprose from her wheel the beautiful
    Puritan maiden,
Pleased with the praise of her thrift from him
    whose praise was the sweetest,

Drew from the reel on the table a snowy skein
   of her spinning,
Thus making answer, meanwhile, to the flattering
   phrases of Alden:
" Come, you must not be idle ; if I am a pattern
   of housewives,
Show yourself equally worthy of being the model
   of husbands.
Hold this skein on your hands while I wind it,
   ready for knitting ;
Then who knows but hereafter, when fashions
   have changed, and the manners,
Fathers may talk to their sons of the good old
   times of John Alden ! "
Thus, with a jest and a laugh, the skein on his
   hands she adjusted,
He sitting awkwardly there, with his arms ex-
   tended before him,
She standing graceful, erect, and winding the
   thread from his fingers,
Sometimes chiding a little his clumsy manner of
   holding,
Sometimes touching his hands, as she dis-
   entangled expertly
Twist or knot in the yarn, unawares, — for how
   could she help it ? —

Sending electrical thrills through every nerve in
his body.

. . . .

Even as rivulets twain, from distant and separate sources,
Seeing each other afar as they leap from the
rocks, and pursuing
Each one its devious path, but drawing nearer
and nearer,
Rush together at last, at their trysting-place in
the forest;
So these lives, that had run thus far in separate
channels,
Coming in sight of each other, then swerving
and flowing asunder,
Parted by barriers strong, but drawing nearer
and nearer,
Rushed together at last, and one was lost in the
other.

THE MARRIAGE.

Forth from the curtain of clouds, from the
tent of purple and scarlet,
Issued the sun, the great high priest, in his garments resplendent;

Holiness unto the Lord, in letters of light, on
his forehead,
Round the hem of his robe the golden bells and
pomegranates.
Blessing the world he came, and the bars of
vapor beneath him
Gleamed like a grate of brass, and the sea at his
feet was a laver !

This was the wedding morn of Priscilla the
Puritan maiden.
Friends were assembled together ; the elder and
magistrate also
Graced the scene with their presence and stood
like the law and the gospel,
One with the sanction of earth and one with the
blessing of heaven.
Simple and brief was the wedding as that of
Ruth and Boaz.
Softly the youth and the maiden repeated the
words of betrothal,
Taking .each other for husband and wife in the
magistrate's presence,
After the Puritan way, and the laudable custom
of Holland.

Fervéntly then, and devoutly, the excellent elder
    of Plymouth
Prayed for the hearth and the home that were
    founded that day in affection,
Speaking of life and of death, and imploring
    divine benedictions.

— H. W. Longfellow.

ON HER MOTHER.

A WORTHY matron of unspotted life,
    A loving mother and obedient wife ;
A friendly neighbor, pitiful to poor,
Whom oft she fed and clothed with her store ;
To servants wisely awful, but yet kind,
And as they did, so they reward did find ;
A true instructor of her family,
The which she ordered with dexterity.
The public meetings ever did frequent,
And in her closet constant hours she spent ;
Religious in all her words and wayes,
Preparing still for death till end of dayes ;
Of all her children, children lived to see ;
Then dying, left a blessed memory.

—Anne Bradstreet.

TWO HUNDRED YEARS AGO.[1]

Special Music.

COME, listen to my story,
　Though often told before,
Of men who passed to glory,
　Through toil and travail sore ;
Of men who did for conscience' sake
　Their native land forego,
And sought a home and freedom here,
　Two hundred years ago.

Oh, 't was no earth-born passion
　That bade the adventurers stray ;
The world and all its fashion
　With them had passed away.
A voice from heaven bade them look
　Above the things below,
When here they sought a resting-place,
　Two hundred years ago.

Oh, dark the scene and dreary,
　When here they set them down,
Of storms and billows weary,
　And chilled with winter's frown,

---

[1] Sung at Plymouth, 22 December, 1820.

Deep moaned the forests to the wind,
   Loud howled the savage foe,
While here their evening prayer arose,
   Two hundred years ago.

'T would drown the heart in sorrow
   To tell of all their woes ;
No respite could they borrow,
   But from the grave's repose.
Yet naught could daunt the Pilgrim Band,
   Or sink their courage low,
Who came to plant the gospel here,
   Two hundred years ago.

With humble prayer and fasting,
   In every strait and grief,
They sought the everlasting,
   And found a sure relief.
Their covenant God o'ershadowed them,
   Their shield from every foe,
And gave them here a dwelling-place,
   Two hundred years ago.

Of fair New England's glory
   They laid the corner-stone ;
This praise, in deathless story,
   Their grateful sons shall own.

Prophetic, they foresaw in time
  A mighty state should grow
From them, a few faint Pilgrims here,
  Two hundred years ago.

If greatness be in daring,
  Our Pilgrim sires were great,
Whose sojourn here, unsparing,
  Disease and famine wait;
And oft their treacherous foes combined
  To lay the strangers low,
While founding here their commonwealth,
  Two hundred years ago.

Though seeming over-zealous
  In things by us deemed light,
They were but duly jealous
  Of power usurping right.
They nobly chose to part with all
  Most dear to men below,
To worship here their God in peace,
  Two hundred years ago.

From seeds they sowed with weeping
  Our richest harvests rise;
We still the fruits are reaping
  Of Pilgrim enterprise.

Then grateful we to them will pay
  The debt of fame we owe,
Who planted here the tree of life,
  Two hundred years ago.

As comes this period yearly,
  Around our cheerful fires,
We 'll think and tell how dearly
  Our comforts cost our sires.
For them we 'll wake the votive song,
  And bid the canvas glow,
Who fixed the home of freedom here,
  Two hundred years ago.
                  — James Flint.

ANNIVERSARY STANZAS.[1]

(1808.)

AH! 't is a barren shore
  To which we go ;
And rough the billows roar,
  And tempests blow !
Poor Pilgrims have we come
Hither to fix our home ;
Or must we farther roam
  Through drifting snow ?

[1] Supposed to be sung by the Pilgrims on arrival.

Songs of the Pilgrims.

No! by this sheltering hill
  A log-house rear:
With clay each crevice fill,
  T" exclude the air:
There covered from the storm,
Our shivering limbs we 'll warm,
And then in ample form
  The feast prepare.

Though scanty be our store,
  And coarse our bread,
The God who heretofore
  Elijah fed
Will pity our distress,
And for our neediness
E'en in the wilderness
  A table spread.

Already he displays
  His bounteous hand,
In hoards of Indian maize
  Beneath the strand.
He fills the empty cruse,
Fine fish these seas produce,
And treasures for our use
  Hides in the sand.

Since thus we freely share
His kind supply,
And on his guardian care
Secure rely,
Still may he succor lend,
And may his grace descend,
Our children to befriend,
When we shall die.

Author Unknown.

———

HYMN.[1]

FATHER supreme of heaven and earth,
Creative Source of all!
Whence infant nations spring to birth,
And empires rise and fall!

Thy throne, above the circling spheres,
Shall stand while centuries roll;
Nor boundless space, nor endless years,
Can limit thy control!

To him from whom our blessings flow,
Who all our wants supplies,
This day the choral song and vow
From grateful hearts shall rise!

[1] Sung at the Albany celebration of 22 December, 1820.

'T was he who led the *Pilgrim band*
  Across the stormy sea ;
'T was he who stayed the tyrant's hand,
  And set our empire free !

When shivering on a strand unknown,
  In sickness and distress,
Our fathers looked to God alone,
  To save, protect, and bless.

Be thou our nation's strength and shield,
  In manhood, as in youth ;
Thine arm for our protection wield,
  And guide us by thy truth !

ODE FOR 22D DECEMBER.

Tune: *St. Martins.*

LET children learn the mighty deeds
  Their sires achieved of old ;
And still, as time to time succeeds,
  To them the tale unfold.

Here while we fondly trace the scene
  This joyous day recalls,
Let youth with reverent age convene
  Within these hallowed walls.

Their pious toils, their just rewards,
  Returning tributes claim,
While faithful history records
  Each venerable name.

Here first the temple's votive fane,
  Aspiring, sought the skies,
And here religion's exiled train
  Bade sacred altars rise.

No longer now the roaming hordes
  Unhallowed vigils keep ;
No more affrighted mothers guard
  Their cradled infants' sleep :

But social arts and peaceful homes
  This favored land endear,
Where fields and masts and rising domes,
  With scattered grace, appear.

Let musing strangers view the ground,
  Here seek tradition's lore,
Where Pilgrims walked on holy ground
  With God in days of yore ;

And where around the savage tribe
  Alarmed with horrid yells,

Assembling crowds secure imbibe
  What holy legend tells.

Let children emulate their deeds,
  Their choral praises sing ;
So shall the Muse, as time proceeds,
  Her meed of incense bring.

                   — *Samuel Davis.*

HYMN.[1]

WHEN Israel's God had marked the way
  From persecution's fiery sway,
Our fathers left their native land,
Sustained by his almighty hand.

His providence their trust and guide,
Securely through the deep they glide ;
A world unknown their hopes explore ;
By faith they reach the promised shore.

Fervent the Christian Pilgrims raise
On heathen soil their shouts of praise ;
With thankful hearts aloud proclaim
In heathen lands Jehovah's name.

[1] Sung at the Albany celebration of 22 December, 1820.

Jehovah's name ! the hills rejoice,
Glad nature owns her Maker's voice ;
The wilderness breaks forth in songs
To him to whom all praise belongs.

Let all their children rise, and bring
Their grateful incense to our King ;
In his fair courts their voices raise,
And fill the land with songs and praise !

SELECTIONS FROM A HYMN.[1]

GOD of our Fathers — Zion's King !
   With eye propitious now behold,
While in thy house thy praise we sing,
And celebrate thy works of old.

Like Israel, our New England sires,
   By cruel persecution driven,
Through dearths and deserts, seas and fires,
   Followed the guiding hand of heaven.

To heaven, their home, their prayer ascends,
   For they were Pilgrims on the earth ;
Exiled from country, kindred, friends,
   They sought the land which gave us birth.

[1] Sung at Haverhill, Mass., 22 December, 1820.

For this they plowed the wintry main,
  And braved the dangers of the deep ;
Cheerful and patient under pain,
  For Christ was with them in the ship.

Now on Columbia's savage coast,
  Escaped from shipwreck and from storm,
Behold the feeble, shivering host —
  Their pious hearts alone were warm.

Heroic souls ! New England's pride !
  For us who could all dangers brave
They toiled, they prayed, they bled, they died —
  Nor found their rest but in the grave.

May we, their sons, thy praise acclaim,
  The God our fathers loved adore ;
Our children's children fear thy name,
  Till suns shall rise and set no more.

———

THAT little Mayflower, conveyed by the winds
    And the rude waters to our rocky shore,
Shall scatter freedom's seed throughout the world;
And all the nations of the earth shall come
Singing to share the harvest-home of truth.[1]

— *Lowell.*

[1] By permission of Houghton, Mifflin & Co.

THE FIRST THANKSGIVING.

(1621.)

EDWARD WINSLOW'S STORY.

WE had gathered in our harvests,
  And stored the yellow grain,
For God had sent the sunshine,
  And sent the plenteous rain ;
Our barley-land and corn-land
  Had yielded up their store,
And the fear and dread of famine
  Oppressed our homes no more.

As the chosen tribes of Israel,
  In the far years of old,
When the summer fruits were garnered,
  And before the winter's cold,
Kept their festal week with gladness,
  With songs and choral lays,
So we kept our first Thanksgiving
  In the hazy autumn days.

Through the mild months of summer,
  We had built us pleasant homes,
So that now we fear no danger,
  When the angry winter comes ;

We can sit by cheerful firesides,
　And watch the flickering ray,
When the storms of ocean gather,
　And howl around the bay.

We think with grief and sadness
　Of the gloomy months gone by,
When want was in our dwellings,
　And we saw our loved ones die ;
But when our well-filled garners
　Moved all our hearts to praise,
We kept our glad Thanksgiving
　In the soft October[1] days.

We sent our keen-eyed gunners
　To the forest-haunts for game,
And with ample wealth of wild fowl,
　Rejoicing home they came ;
And our good Indian neighbors,
　With whom we live in peace,
Brought in their gift of hunted deer,
　Our larder to increase.

[1] Mr. Tarbox thinks it probable that the first Thanksgiving took place in October. See article in New England for March, 1879.

And Massasoit, the chieftain,
　Was present with us then ;
He came to share our banquet,
　With his ninety dusky men ;
So for three days we feasted,
　With sports, and games, and plays,
And kept our first Thanksgiving
　In the fair autumnal days.

The winds breathed gently on us
　From out the mild south-west ;
They come, the Indians tell us,
　From the islands of the blest ;
And the sun and moon looked kindly
　From the still heights above,
As if to cheer our banquet,
　And bless our feast of love.

And our brave Captain Standish,
　Brought up 'mid war's alarms,
Led out his small but trusty band,
　His sturdy men-at-arms ;
He showed the Indian warriors
　Our military ways ;
For so we kept Thanksgiving
　In those hazy autumn days.

We thought of dear old England,
  Dear, though to us unkind ;
Of the fond familiar faces
  That we had left behind ;
But England can not wean us
  Back from our forest home,
Where we lay our sure foundations
  For the better years to come.

So we passed the days in gladness,
  In social joy and mirth,
As those who have their dwelling-place
  As yet upon the earth ;
But to the Lord our God we brought
  Our gifts of prayer and praise ;
So we kept our first Thanksgiving
  In the dreamy autumn days.
                    — *Increase N. Tarbox.*

THE FIRST THANKSGIVING DAY.
A.D. 1622.

A ND now," said the governor, gazing abroad
  on the piled-up store
Of the sheaves that dotted the clearings and
  covered the meadows o'er,

" 'T is meet that we render praises because of
    this yield of grain ;
'T is meet that the Lord of the harvest be
    thanked for his sun and rain.

" And therefore, I, William Bradford (by the
    grace of God to-day,
And the franchise of this good people), gov-
    ernor of Plymouth, say, —
Through virtue of vested power, — ye shall
    gather with one accord
And hold, in the month of November, Thanks-
    giving unto the Lord.

" He hath granted us peace and plenty, and the
    quiet we 've sought so long ;
He hath thwarted the wily savage, and kept him
    from wrack and wrong :
And unto our feast the sachem shall be bidden,
    that he may know
We worship his own Great Spirit, who maketh
    the harvests grow.

" So shoulder your matchlocks, masters ; there
    is hunting of all degrees ;
And fishermen, take your tackle and scour for
    spoil the seas ;

And maidens and dames of Plymouth, your
　　delicate crafts employ
To honor our first Thanksgiving, and make it a
　　feast of joy!

" We fail of the fruits and dainties, we fail of
　　the old home cheer;
Ah! these are the lightest losses, mayhap, that
　　befall us here.
But see! in our open clearings how golden the
　　melons lie!
Enrich them with sweets and spices, and give us
　　the pumpkin-pie!"

So, bravely the preparations went on for the
　　autumn feast:
The deer and the bear were slaughtered; wild
　　game from the greatest to least
Was heaped in the colony cabins; brown home-
　　brew served for wine;
And the plum and the grape of the forest for
　　orange and peach and pine.

At length came the day appointed; the snow
　　had begun to fall,
But the clang of the meeting-house belfry rang
　　merrily over all,

And summoned the folk of Plymouth, who has-
    tened with glad accord
To listen to Elder Brewster as he fervently
    thanked the Lord.

In his seat sate Governor Bradford ; men, ma-
    trons, and maidens fair ;
Miles Standish and all his soldiers, with corslet
    and sword were there ;
And sobbing and tears and gladness had each in
    its turn the sway,
For the grave of sweet Rose Standish o'ershad-
    owed Thanksgiving day.

And when Massasoit, the sachem, sate down
    with his hundred braves,
And ate of the varied riches of gardens and
    woods and waves,
And looked on the granaried harvest, with a
    blow on his brawny chest,
He muttered : " The Good Spirit loves his white
    children best ! "

                          — *Margaret J. Preston.*

ODE.[1]

THE Pilgrim Fathers — where are they?
   The waves that brought them o'er
Still roll in the bay, and throw their spray
   As they break along the shore ;
Still roll in the bay as they rolled that day
   When the Mayflower moored below,
When the sea around was black with storms,
   And white the shore with snow.

The mists that wrapped the Pilgrims' sleep
   Still brood upon the tide ;
And his rocks yet keep their watch by the deep,
   To stay its waves of pride ;
But the snow-white sail, that he gave to the
     gale
When the heavens looked dark, is gone :
As an angel's wing, through an opening cloud
   Is seen, and then withdrawn.

The Pilgrim exile — sainted name !
   The hill, whose icy brow
Rejoiced, when he came, in the morning's flame,
   In the morning's flame burns now.

---

[1] For the celebration of 22 December, 1824.

And the moon's cold light as it lay that night,
On the hill-side and the sea,
Still lies where he laid his houseless head ;
But the Pilgrim — where is he?

The Pilgrim Fathers are at rest.
When summer 's throned on high,
And the world's warm breast is in verdure
dressed,
Go, stand on the hill where they lie.
The earliest ray of the golden day
On that hallowed spot is cast ;
And the evening sun, as he leaves the world,
Looks kindly on that spot last.

The Pilgrim *spirit* has not fled :
It walks in noon's broad light ;
And it watches the bed of the glorious dead,
With the holy stars by night.
It watches the bed of the brave who have
bled,
And shall guard this ice-bound shore,
Till the waves of the bay where the Mayflower
lay
Shall foam and freeze no more.

— John Pierpont.

HYMN.[1]

Tune: *Scots, wha ha'.*

HOLY spot! where glowing choirs
Oft have wakened grateful lyres,
Oft have kindled grateful fires,
O'er the Pilgrim's grave.

Once again we press the shore
Where our fathers sternly swore
Ocean should forget to roar,
Ere they would be slaves.

Hail the dawn when Freedom's rays
Hushed Columbia's icy face,
Sweeter strains arise of praise
Than from Memnon's harp.

Hail the spot — our sires' retreat!
Hail the waves that round them beat!
Hail the rock that bore their feet,
When their wanderings ceased!

Fancy paints in yonder bay
The bark that broke the Pilgrims' way,
The cradle where our nation lay
In her infant days.

[1] Sung at Pilgrim Hall at the celebration of 1824.

See the boat approach the land,
Freighted with the pious band,
See, they kneel upon the strand,
 Warm with gratitude.

Vent your fury, wind and flood,
Freedom's bark is safely moored,
Freedom's sons with hearts assured,
 Now their work begin.

Gloomy scenes await the brave;
Savage foes around them rave;
Carver fills an early grave;
 Hope well-nigh expires.

But to Faith's reluming eye,
Visions bright in prospect lie;
E'en a triumph 't were to die,
 If in conscience free.

Still above the sacred dead,
Future crowds shall yearly tread;
Blooming youth and hoary head
 Meet around their urns.

Oft shall Genius' fluent tongue
Trace the story, swell the song;
Oft amidst the listening throng
 Thrill the feeling soul.

Ye who 've sprung from noble blood,
Men who spurned the tyrant's rod,
Men who bowed to none but God,
    Here your vows repeat :

" By their pious shades we swear,   .
By their toils and perils here,
We will guard with jealous care
    Law and Liberty."
           — *William P. Lunt.*

THE TWENTY-SECOND OF DECEMBER.

(1829.)

WILD was the day ; the wintry sea
    Moaned sadly on New England's strand,
When first the thoughtful and the free,
Our fathers, trod the desert land.

They little thought how pure a light,
With years, should gather round that day ;
How love should keep their memories bright,
How wide a realm their sons should sway.

Green are their bays ; but greener still
    Shall round their spreading fame be wreathed,
And regions, now untold, shall thrill
    With   reverence,   when   their   names   are
        breathed.

Till where the sun, with softer fires,
    Looks on the vast Pacific's sleep,
The children of the Pilgrim sires
    This hallowed day like us shall keep.
               — William Cullen Bryant.

ORIGINAL HYMN.

LONG persecuted and oppressed,
    The exiled Pilgrim band,
In search of liberty and rest,
    Came to a desert land.

God deigned their enterprise to bless,
    And gave the wished repose ;
And, glad for them. the wilderness
    Soon blossomed as the rose.

Schools, churches, and the ministry
　Their earliest cares engage ;
The glory of their times to be,
　And of each coming age.

The benefits which hence arise,
　On us heaven kindly showers,
And shows us, by the rich supplies,
　Our fathers' God is ours.
　　　　　　— Thaddeus Mason Harris.

THE PRICE OF A LITTLE PILGRIM.

(A.D. 1621.)

GO, wind the signal-horn, and bid
　　My band of trusty men
Come stern and grim, in fighting trim,
　That I may choose me ten.

" They may not wait to kiss their wives,
　For there 's a life at cost, —
A tender one, — the widow's son,
　Ralf Billington, is lost ;

"The pretty lad that often drew
　My sword, and vowed that yet
He 'd march away some summer day
　And capture Aspinet."

So spake the Plymouth governor,
　And at the signal sound
Forth came the band at his command,
　And crowded eager round.

" Ten only," Governor Bradford said,
　" Will fill the boat enow ;
I want but ten strong-handed men,
　Now which of you will go ? "

They shouted, " I ! " " And I ! " " And I ! "
　" Nay, hold ! " he bade, " I 'll find
Some Gideon test to mark the best ;
　The rest shall bide behind.

"Ye who are fathers, — ye whose homes
　Are glad with children's joy, —
Your quest, I wot, will slacken not,
　Till ye have found the boy."

The shallop manned, they searched the coast,
　They beat the tangled wild ;
And sought to trace, in many a place,
　Some tidings of the child.

They steered through silent, sheltered coves,
  They skimmed the marshes wide;
And all around the shallows wound,
  With Squanto for their guide.

At length they saw a curl of smoke
  Float o'er the distant trees;
And all about, the whoop and shout
  Came blown upon the breeze.

Scarce had they landed, when the cry
  Of " Yengese ! " rent the air;
And even before they touched the shore,
  The foe was yelling there,

Each with his arrow drawn to head.
  " Stay ! stay ! " cried Squanto, " Let
True braves be friends ; our sachem sends
  To you his calumet.

" The mother in her wigwam weeps,
  Bereft of peace and joy;
Now we would know if it be so
  That ye have found her boy ? "

" Ugh ! " growled the wily Aspinet;
  " What will the Yengese grant,
If I set loose the white papoose,
  And bring him from Nahant ? "

" Name what ye will ! " the captain cried,
  " So much we prize his life ! "
The sachem heard, and with brief word
  Muttered, " A knife ! a knife ! "

" Good ! " and the captain grimly smiled
  Aside ; " and yet I trow
The dame will be scarce pleased that we
  Should rate her boy so low !

" Go, Squanto, hither fetch the lad ;
  And lest it will not do,
For one jack-knife to buy a life,
  Why, Squanto, give him two ! "
                              — *Margaret J. Preston.*

THE LANDING OF THE PILGRIM FATHERS.

THE breaking waves dashed high
  On a stern and rock-bound coast,
And the woods, against a stormy sky,
  Their giant branches tossed ;

And the heavy night hung dark,
  The hills and waters o'er,
When a band of exiles moored their bark
  On the wild New England shore.

Not as the conqueror comes,
  They, the true hearted, came ;
Not with the roll of the stirring drums,
  And the trumpet that sings of fame ;

Not as the flying come,
  In silence and in fear !
They shook the depths of the desert's gloom
  With their hymns of lofty cheer.

Amidst the storm they sang,
  And the stars heard, and the sea !
And the sounding aisles of the dim woods rang
  To the anthem of the free !

The ocean-eagle soared
  From his nest by the white wave's foam,
And the rocking pines of the forest roared —
  This was their welcome home !

There were men with hoary hair,
  Amidst that Pilgrim band ;
Why had they come to wither there,
  Away from their childhood's land ?

There was woman's fearless eye,
  Lit by her deep love's truth ;
There was manhood's brow serenely high,
  And the fiery heart of youth.

What sought they thus afar?
  Bright jewels of the mine?
The wealth of seas, the spoils of war? —
  They sought a faith's pure shrine !

Ay ! call it holy ground,
  The soil where first they trod !
They have left unstained what there they found,
  Freedom to worship God !

              — Mrs. Felicia Hemans.

NEW ENGLAND.

HAIL to the land whereon we tread,
  Our fondest boast ;
The sepulcher of mighty dead,
The truest hearts that ever bled,
Who sleep on glory's brightest bed,
  A fearless host.

No slave is here ; our unchained feet
Walk freely as the waves that beat
    Our coast.

Our fathers crossed the ocean's wave
    To seek this shore ;
They left behind the coward slave
To welter in his living grave ;
With hearts unbent, and spirits brave,
    They sternly bore
Such toils as meaner souls had quelled,
But souls like these such toils impelled
    To soar.

.   .   .   .

There is no other land like thee,
    No dearer shore ;
Thou art the shelter of the free ;
The home, the port of Liberty,
Thou hast been, and shalt ever be,
    Till time is o'er.
Ere I forget to think upon
My land, shall mother curse the son
    She bore.

                —*J. G. Percival.*

THE FIRST PROCLAMATION OF MILES STANDISH.

(November, A.D. 1620.)

H O!" quoth the stout Miles Standish,
　　As he stood on the Mayflower's deck,
And gazed on the sandy coast-line,
　　That loomed as a misty speck

On the edge of the distant offing, —
　　" See! yonder we have in view
Bartholomew Gosnold's headlands.
　　'T was in sixteen hundred and two

"That the Concord of Dartmouth anchored
　　Just there where the beach is broad,
And the merry old captain named it
　　(Half-swamped by the fish) Cape Cod.

"And so, as his mighty headlands
　　Are scarcely a league away,
What say you to landing, Sweetheart,
　　And having a washing-day?

"For did not the mighty leader,
　　Who guided the chosen band,
Pause under the peaks of Sinai,
　　And issue his strict command

" (For even the least assoilment
    Of Egypt the Spirit loathes),
Or ever they entered Canaan,
    The people should wash their clothes?

"The land we have left is noisome,
    And rank with the smirch of sin;
The land that we seek should find us
    Clear-vestured without and within."

Dear heart — and the sweet Rose Standish
    Looked up with a tear in her eye;
She was back in the flag-stoned kitchen
    Where she watched, in the days gone by,

Her mother among her maidens
    (She should watch them no more, alas!),
And saw as they stretched the linen
    To bleach on the Suffolk grass.

In a moment her brow was cloudless,
    As she leaned on the vessel's rail,
And thought of the sea-stained garments,
    Of coif, and of farthingale;

And the doublets of fine Welsh flannel,
    The tuckers and homespun gowns,
And the piles of the hosen knitted
    From the wool of the Devon Downs.

So the matrons aboard the Mayflower
　Made ready with eager hand
To drop from the deck their baskets
　As soon as the prow touched land.

And there did the Pilgrim mothers,
　On a Monday, the record says,
Ordain for their new-found England
　The first of her washing-days.

And there did the Pilgrim fathers,
　With matchlock and axe well slung,
Keep guard o'er the smoking kettles
　That propt on the crotchets hung.

For the trail of the startled savage
　Was over the marshy grass,
And the glint of his eyes kept peering
　Through cedar and sassafras.

And the children were mad with pleasure
　As they gathered the twigs in sheaves,
And piled on the fire the fagots,
　And heaped up the autumn leaves.

Do the thing that is next, saith the proverb,
　And a nobler shall yet succeed :
'T is the motive exalts the action ;
　'T is the doing, and not the deed :

For the earliest act of the heroes
　　Whose fame has a world-wide sway
Was — to fashion a crane for a kettle,
　　And order a washing-day !
　　　　　　　— *Margaret J. Preston.*

THE PILGRIMS' DAY.[1]

WITH joy I heard them say
　　When roving far abroad,
On this their landing-day
　　We 'll praise the Pilgrims' God.
　　　　I knew the cry,
　　　I 'll join the song,
　　　Thy courts we 'll throng,
　　　　O Thou most high !

This day let all awake,
　.　And sing the mighty dead
Who, first, for Zion's sake,
　　O'er raging oceans fled.
　　　　Had not our God
　　　Preserved that flock,
　　　Safe on the rock
　　　　They ne'er had trod.

[1] By a member of the New England Society of New York.

At once their temples rose,
  Our schools were founded then,
Nor could their mightier foes
  Withstand those valiant men :
    But vain their skill,
And vain their sword,
Had not the Lord
    Upheld them still.

Peace to that holy ground !
  That consecrated spot !
The first our fathers found
  Where tyrants trouble not.
    We 'll sound abroad,
Where'er we roam,
The Pilgrims' home,
    The Pilgrims' God.

ODE.[1]

Tune: *America.*

SONS of New England sires !
  Why do your altar-fires
Flame up on high ;

[1] For the 34th Anniversary of the New England Society.

Why from your festal board
Wakes the loud anthem, pour'd
Joyous, with one accord,
    Winged for the sky?

Not for the voice that spoke
Triumph, when Britain's yoke
    Burst with your chains ;
Not for the heroes brave,
Bleeding by Charles's wave,
Not for the patriots' grave,
    Wake ye your strains ;

But for the Pilgrim band,
They who from Leyden's land
    Dared the rough sea ;
Braving the ocean vast,
Scorning the wintry blast,
So they might find, at last,
    Room for the free.

Hark, how the thunder peals !
See, how the brave ship reels,
    Whirled in the brine !
Courage ! the God that wears
Storm-robes, the good man spares.
Pilgrim ! he hears your prayers,
    Joy to your line !

Nobly the Mayflower bows,
While the dark wave she plows
    On to the West;
Till, from the tempest's shock,
Proudly she lands her flock,
Where on old Plymouth Rock,
    Freedom found rest.

Lo! from yon starry sphere,
Spirits in light appear,
    Glorious, but few.
Pilgrims! we see you now,
Fathers! to you we bow,
Hear, then, your children's vow,
    Still to be true.

Join, brothers, heart and hand,
Sons of the Pilgrim band!
    Swear now to be
All that your fathers sought,
All that their virtue wrought,
So shall your sons be taught
    How to be free!

            — Rufus Dawes.

THE PILGRIM FATHERS: AN ODE.

THEY come — that coming who shall tell?
     The eye may weep, the heart may swell,
But the poor tongue in vain essays
A fitting note for them to raise.
We hear the after-shout that rings
For them who smote the power of kings;
The swelling triumph all would share;
But who the dark defeat would dare,
And boldly meet the wrath and woe
That wait the unsuccessful blow?
It were an envied fate, we deem,
To live a land's recorded theme,
     When we are in the tomb.
We, too, might yield the joys of home,
And waves of winter darkness roam,
     And tread a shore of bloom,

Knew we those waves, through coming time,
Should roll our names to every clime;
Felt we that millions on that shore
Should stand, our memory to adore.
But no glad vision burst in light
Upon the Pilgrims' aching sight;

Their hearts no proud hereafter swelled ;
Deep shadows veiled the way they held ;
The yell of vengeance was their trump of fame ;
Their monument — a grave without a name.

Yet, strong in weakness, there they stand,
　On yonder ice-bound Rock,
Stern and resolved, that faithful band,
　To meet fate's rudest shock.

Though anguish rends the father's breast,
For them, his dearest and his best,
　With him the waste who trod ;
Though tears that freeze, the mother sheds,
Upon her children's houseless heads,
　The Christian turns to God.

In grateful adoration now
Upon the barren sands they bow.
What tongue of joy e'er woke such prayer
As bursts in desolation there?
What arm of strength e'er wrought such power
As waits to crown that feeble hour?
　There into life an infant empire springs ;
There falls the iron from the soul ;
There Liberty's young accents roll
　Up to the King of kings.

To fair creation's farthest bound
That thrilling summons yet shall sound ;
The dreaming nations shall awake,
And to their center earth's old kingdoms shake.
Pontiff and prince, your sway
Must crumble from that day ;
Before the loftier throne of heaven
The hand is raised, the pledge is given,
One monarch to obey, one creed to own —
That monarch, God, that creed, his Word alone.

Spread out earth's holiest records here,
Of days and deeds to reverence dear ;
A zeal like this what pious legends tell !
   On kingdoms built
   In blood and guilt,   .
The worshipers of vulgar triumph dwell !
 But what exploits with theirs shall page
Who rose to bless their kind,
 Who left their nation and their age
Man's spirit to unbind !
 Who boundless seas passed o'er,
And boldly met, in every path,
Famine, and frost, and heathen wrath,
 To dedicate a shore

Where Piety's meek train might breathe their
    vow,
And seek their Maker with an unshamed brow ;
Where Liberty's glad race might proudly come,
And set up there an everlasting home !
Oh, many a time it hath been told,
The story of those men of old.
For this fair Poetry hath wreathed
    Her sweetest, purest flower ;
For this proud Eloquence hath breathed
    His strain of loftiest power ;
Devotion, too, hath lingered round
Each spot of consecrated ground,
    And hill and valley blessed ;
There, where our banished fathers strayed,
There, where they loved, and wept, and prayed,
    There, where their ashes rest.

And never may they rest unsung
While Liberty can find a tongue.
Twine, Gratitude, a wreath for them,
More deathless than the diadem,
    Who to life's noblest end
        Gave up life's noblest powers,
    And bade the legacy descend
        Down, down to us and ours !
                    Charles Sprague.

THE PILGRIM MOTHERS.

THE sculptor's art has striv'n
 And bards have strung their lyres
To celebrate the deeds
 Of our brave Pilgrim *sires;*

But written in the sand,
 As fleeting their few names,
The virtues who shall paint
 Of our meek Pilgrim *dames?*

Wife, widow, matron, maid —
 Who braved the stormy sea,
And worthy to become
 The *mothers* of the free !

With their more hardy mates —
 Age leaning upon youth,
From whose soft eyes beamed forth
 The soul of love and truth !

And when the Mayflower's bark
 Neared the unfriendly strand,
Was not a *woman* first
 Upon the ROCK to land?

While later o'er the deep,
　Her infant by her side,
Sweet ALICE SOUTHWORTH came
　To be the Governor's bride.

As from the vessel's side
　The Pilgrims disembark,
Borne o'er the waves dry shod,
　Religion's sacred ark,

So, hallowed by their feet
　Yon islet at length trod,
The Lord's day first they spent
　In prayer and praise to God ;

Then sent a chosen few
　Each inlet to explore,
And find a place to land
　Upon the hostile shore.

MILES STANDISH — captain bold,
　Who was no carpet knight,
And modest still as brave, —
　A hero in the fight, —

(Whose " Courtship " our loved bard
　So quaintly could rehearse,
Its memory enshrined
　In his idyllic verse,

And tell by proxy how
   JOHN ALDEN ill had sped
His wooing, who, maid's wit,
   PRISCILLA MULLINS wed),

First offering thanks to God
   Upon his bended knee,
With grave and anxious mien
   Supporting tenderly

A woman's fragile form,
   Amid December's snows,
Transferred to alien soil —
   New England's loveliest ROSE !

Around whose rugged stem
   Its tendrils close entwine,
Grace wedded still with strength,
   The oak clasped by the vine.

Vain were it, too, to tell
   Of that *first winter* dread,
When scarce enough survived
   E'en to inter the dead.

With pining want and pain
   And sickness oft laid low ;
Assailed by savage beasts,
   And the more savage foe.

When CARVER first of all —
  Who led the little band,
The pillar of the state —
  Went to the better land,

With " Elder BREWSTER," sage,
  Whose " Chair " too we revere.
Next, BRADFORD, annalist,
  Its chief who knew no fear !

So, let the shaft arise,
  Of native granite wrought,
To our brave sires devote,
  And lofty as their thought,

Upon yon windy height,
  With pious tears besprent,
Which speaks of faith and hope —
  The PILGRIMS' MONUMENT !

Nor less the *gentler sex*,
  In modest garb arrayed,
Who both could " toil " and " spin,"
  The matron and the maid.

The " age of homespun " theirs,
  Of which we glibly prate,
Whose virtues — " *homespun*," too —
  We well may imitate !

On that lone ancient hill
  Whose base the ocean laves,
Concealed from friend or foe,
  They sleep in " unmarked graves."

Save the few spirits rare
  Whose names to our lips rise,
Who live to bless the race
  With loving ministries ;

Before whose luster bright
  The warrior's glory pales :
The CLARA BARTONS famed,
  Or FLORENCE NIGHTINGALES !

With anthem and with psalm
  So celebrate their worth —
The heroines whose type
  Is perished from the earth !

God of our Pilgrim *sires*,
  For their faith we praise thee !
Joined with our Pilgrim *dames*,
  Through blest eternity !
                              — *E. W. Robbins.*

SONG OF THE PILGRIMS.

THE breeze has swelled the whitening sail,
  The blue waves curl beneath the gale,
And, bounding with the wave and wind,
We leave old England's shores behind.
    Leave behind our native shore,
    Homes, and all we loved before.

The deep may dash, the winds may blow,
The storm spread out its wings of woe,
Till sailors' eyes can see a shroud
Hung in the folds of every cloud;
    Still, as long as life shall last,
    From that shore we 'll speed us fast.

For we would rather never be,
Than dwell where mind can not be free,
But bows beneath a despot's rod
Even where it seeks to worship God.
    Blasts of heaven, onward sweep!
    Bear us o'er the troubled deep!

Oh, see what wonders meet our eyes!
Another land, and other skies!
Columbian hills have met our view!

Adieu! Old England's shores, adieu!
  Here, at length, our feet shall rest,
  Hearts be free, and homes be blessed.

As long as yonder firs shall spread
Their green arms o'er the mountain's head —
As long as yonder cliffs shall stand,
Where join the ocean and the land —
  Shall those cliffs and mountains be
  Proud retreats for liberty.

Now to the King of kings we 'll raise
The pæan loud of sacred praise ;
More loud than sounds the swelling breeze,
More loud than speak the rolling seas!
  Happier lands have met our view!
  England's shores, adieu! adieu!

              — *T. C. Upham.*

THE MAYFLOWER.

O LITTLE fleet! that on thy quest divine
    Sailedst from Palos one bright autumn
      morn,
Say, has old Ocean's bosom ever borne
A freight of Faith and Hope to match with thine?

Say, too, has heaven's high favor given again
Such consummation of desire as shone
About Columbus, when he rested on
The new-found world, and married it to Spain?

Answer, thou refuge of the freeman's need,
Thou for whose destinies no kings looked out,
Nor sages to resolve some mighty doubt,
Thou simple Mayflower of the salt sea mead!

When thou wert wafted to that distant shore,
Gay flowers, bright birds, rich odors, met thee
    not;
Stern nature hailed thee to a sterner lot,
God gave free earth and air, and gave no more.

Thus to men cast in that heroic mold
Came empire such as Spaniard never knew,
Such empire as beseems the just and true;
And, at the last, almost unsought, came gold.

But He who rules both calm and stormy days
Can guard that people's heart, that nation's
    health,
Safe on the perilous heights of power and
    wealth,
As in the straitness of the ancient ways.
           — *Lord Houghton.*

HYMN.[1]

Tune: *Tamworth.*

LO! the rising star of Freedom
    Once our Pilgrim Fathers blest;
By her light ordained to lead them
    To the land of promised rest.
        Star of heaven!
        Star of heaven!
Traveling towards the distant West.

While their countless toils enduring,
    Faith the promise kept in sight;
For themselves and sons securing
    Home and country, truth and light.
        Star of heaven!
        Star of heaven!
Pointing to Jehovah's might.

Now the relics round us lying,
    Grateful children guard their clay!
While their spirits, never dying,
    Hope has borne on wings away.
        Star of heaven!
        Star of heaven!
Guiding to a brighter day.

[1] For 22 December, 1831.

Raise we honors to their merit,
  Temples sculptured with their name?
No! their virtues to inherit,
  Seals their bright and conscious fame.
        Star of heaven!
        Star of heaven!
High they shine with ceaseless flame.

See the lights around us gleaming,
  Still to guide the pilgrim's eyes;
See the star of empire beaming,
  Bids their children's glory rise!
        Star of heaven!
        Star of heaven!
Glowing still in Western skies.

                    — *Samuel Deane.*

ST. BOTOLPH'S CHIMES.
(A.D. 1640.)

A PURITAN AND HIS LITTLE DAUGHTER SPEAK ON
THEIR CHURCHWARD WAY.

O father, I wish I could go to church
    As we did in the dear old times,
When we waited to hear the Sunday cheer
    Of St. Botolph's morning chimes!

'T was lovely to walk through the leafy lanes
   In the beautiful English May ;
And I marvel now, as I think of it, how
   You ever could come away.

I want to go back to my oaken seat,
   Where the great round oriel shed
Its crimsons and blues and golden hues,
   All over my hands and head.

As I watched their glory, the service seemed
   So holy and rich and bright !
How tender the glow beside this snow,
   All sheeted and dead and white !

And the carbines, father ; they only hung,
   At home, in the great oak hall ;
Here, we take them abroad to the house of God,
   Yet shiver with fear, for all !

Oh, to mix with the crowd in the dear old street,
   In safety and warmth and ease !
Oh, to wait for the swells of St. Botolph's bells,
   In Boston beyond the seas !

Nay, daughter ! It irks my heart to hear
   Thee hanker as those of old,
With tears on thy cheeks, for Egyptian leeks,
   Because thou art scared and cold.

Why, where is the hero-spirit, child?
  Thy mother forsook her Devon
For an exile here, with a trust as clear
  As if she were going to heaven!

Yea, over thy face the oriel's glint
  Might shimmer with warming glow;
But for me the touch of the priestly clutch
  Was chiller than Shawmut's snow!

I 'm willing to fight for leave to pray,
  And wade with my carbine slung
On my shoulder, and so all chimes forego
  St. Botolph hath ever rung,

To carry thee thus to church to-day,
  As stoutly my strong arm can,
And order my faith as my conscience saith,
  A free and a fearless man!

But, sweetheart, patiently thou must wait,
  For I dream of an end of pains,
In which thou shalt walk in tender talk,
  Through better than English lanes,

With comrades as kind as ever strayed
  Beside thee o'er Lincoln leas,
Or listened betimes to St. Botolph's chimes,
  In Boston beyond the seas!
                              — *Margaret J. Preston.*

ANNIVERSARY HYMN.[1]

Tune: *St. Martins.*

LO! where of old the fathers dwelt,
  From home and temples dear,
And oft in prayer devoutly knelt,
  Their children would appear.

And round thine altar, God of grace!
  With reverent homage stand,
Through ages past thy love to trace
  In this our favored land.

By faith inspired with steadfast mind,
  To shun oppression's rage,
The Pilgrims here their steps inclined,
  Bright heralds of their age.

No golden mines their visions lured,
  No conqueror's pride was theirs;
The soul's pure worship once secured,
  Repays their generous cares.

Here Freedom's sacred altars rose,
  Reared by the Pilgrim sires;
We'll guard them still from threatening foes,
  And light anew their fires.

[1] For the celebration 22 December, 1834.

Great God ! thine all-pervading sway,
   Each passing age controls.
Oh, may thy grace illume our day,
   And ever cheer our souls !
              — *William S. Russell.*

THE MEN OF PLYMOUTH.[1]

THESE are the iron men that broke
   Ground, where the Indian's war-fire curled ;
These spurned the princely, priestly yoke,
   These are the fathers of a world.
O men of God's own image, say !
Can glorious men thus pass away?

No, never ! Send expansive sight !
   From Labrador to Carib's Sea —
That vision, so sublime and bright,
   Of regions teeming with the free,
Shows but the influence of these men
Who sought the sands of Plymouth then.

[1] An extract from a longer poem. 1836.

No, never! Each traditional spot
　Tells where they wept, or sank to rest;
Yet were such silent, or forgot
　The place their Pilgrim footsteps pressed,
Their names should live, nor Time would mock
　The record of the Plymouth Rock.

— William B. Tappan.

FOR FOREFATHERS' DAY.

Tune: *Old Hundred.*

O God! beneath thy guiding hand,
　Our exiled fathers crossed the sea;
And when they trod the wintry strand,
　With prayer and psalm they worshiped thee.

Thou heard'st, well pleased, the song, the prayer,
　Thy blessing came; and still its power
Shall onward to all ages bear
　The memory of that holy hour.

What change !   Through pathless wilds no more
   The fierce and naked savage roams ;
Sweet praise, along the cultured shore,
   Breaks from ten thousand happy homes.

Lands, freedom, truth, and faith in God
  ' Came with those exiles o'er the waves ;
And where their Pilgrim feet have trod,
   The God they trusted guards their graves.

And here thy name, O God of love !
   Their children's children shall adore,
Till these eternal hills remove,
   And spring adorns the earth no more.
                       — *Leonard Bacon.*

ODE.

NEW ENGLAND ! receive the heart's trib-
    ute that comes
 - From thine own Pilgrim sons far away.
More fondly than ever our thoughts turn to thee,
   Upon this thine old festival day.
We would rescue with social observance and
    song,

Awhile from oblivion's grave,
The loved scenes of our youth, and those bless-
          ings recall
Which our country and forefathers gave.

.   .   .   .

Can distance efface, or can time ever dim
     Remembrances crowding like these?
They have grown with our growth, and have
          ministered strength,
     As the roots send up life to the trees.
Then be honored the day when the Mayflower
          came,
     And honored the charge that she bore,
The stern, the religious, the glorious men,
     Whom she set on our rough native shore.

New England, advance in thine onward career,
     With thine inborn, all-conquering will:
Still triumph o'er nature's unkindliest form
     By thine energy, patience, and skill.
Thou shalt grow to thy height as thou ever hast
          grown,
     O'er the storms of ephemeral strife,
And thy spirit, undying, shall cease not to be
     The deep germ of a continent's life.
                              — *Samuel Gilman.*

BURIAL HILL.[1]

THEY in storms of dark December,
    Scions of a martyr stock,
Praised the Lord for all his mercies,
    Kneeling there upon the rock.

Praised him while the blast was roaring,
    While the surges smote the strand ;
Praised him while their hearts were yearning
    With their love for fatherland.

In the wilds of death they wrestled,
    Seeking what by faith they saw ;
" Little matter what they died on —
    Beds of down, or locks of straw."

Little recked they pain or peril,
    Ocean wave or scaffold block,
They who bore the name of Pilgrim,
    They who built upon the rock.

For afar they caught a vision —
    Morning merging into noon ;
Snow-wreaths melting into blossoms,
    Dark December changed to June.

John Milton Holmes.

[1] From a longer poem. 1865.

THE PILGRIM'S VISION.[1]

IN the hour of twilight shadows,
  The Puritan looked out ;
He thought of the " bloody savages "
  That lurked all round about,
Of Wituwamut's pictured knife,
  And Pecksvot's whooping shout ;
For the baby's flesh was tender,
  Though his father's arms were stout.

His home was a freezing cabin,
  Too bare for the hungry rat ;
Its roof was thatched with ragged grass,
  And bald enough of that.
The hole that served for casement.
  Was glazed with an ancient hat ;
And the ice was gently thawing
  From the log whereon he sat.

Along the dreary landscape,
  His eyes went to and fro ;
The trees all clad in icicles,
  The streams that did not flow.

[1] For the Plymouth celebration, 22 December, 1846.

A sudden thought flashed o'er him —
    A dream of long ago —
He smote his leathern jerkin,
    And murmured, "Even so!"

"Come hither, God-be-glorified,
    And sit upon my knee;
Behold the dream unfolding,
    Whereof I spake to thee
By the winter's hearth, in Leyden,
    And on the stormy sea;
True is the dream's beginning,
    So may its ending be!

"I saw in the naked forest,
    Our scattered remnant cast;
A screen of shivering branches
    Between them and the blast;
The snow was falling round them,
    The dying fell as fast;
I looked to see them perish,
    When, lo! the vision passed.

"Again mine eyes were opened,
    The feeble had waxed strong;
The babes had grown to sturdy men,
    The remnant was a throng.

By shadowed lake and winding stream,
    And all the shores along,
The howling demons quaked to hear
    The Christian's godly song.

"They slept, the village fathers,
    By river, lake, and shore;
When, far adown the steep of time,
    The vision rose once more.
I saw, along the winter snow,
    A spectral column pour;
And, high above their broken ranks,
    A tattered flag they bore.

"Their leader rode before them,
    Of bearing calm and high;
The light of heaven's own kindling
    Throned in his awful eye.
These were a nation's champions,
    Her dread appeal to try;
God for the right! I faltered,
    And lo! the train passed by.

"Once more, the strife was ended,
    The solemn issue tried;
The Lord of hosts, his mighty arm
    Had helped our Israel's side.

Gray stone and grassy hillock
　　Told where the martyrs died ;
And peace was in the borders
　　Of Victory's chosen bride.

" A crash, as when some swollen cloud
　　Cracks o'er the tangled trees !
With side to side, and spar to spar,
　　Whose smoking decks are these?
I know St. George's blood-red cross,
　　Thou Mistress of the seas,
But who is she whose streaming bars
　　Roll out before the breeze?

" Ah, well her iron ribs are knit,
　　Whose thunders try to quell
The bellowing throats, the blazing lips
　　That pealed the Armada's knell !
The mist was cleared, a wreath of stars
　　Rose o'er the crimsoned swell,
And wavering from its haughty peak,
　　The cross of England fell !

" Oh, trembling Faith ! though dark the morn,
　　A heavenly torch is thine ;
While feebler races melt away
　　And paler orbs decline,

Shall still the fiery pillar's ray
   Along thy pathway shine,
To light the chosen tribe that sought
   This Western Palestine.

"I see the living tide roll on,
   It crowns with flaming towers
The icy cape of Labrador,
   The Spaniard's ' land of flowers.'
It streams beyond the splintered ridge
   That parts the Northern shores,
From Eastern rock to sunset wave
   The continent is ours!"

He ceased, the grim old Puritan,
   Then softly bent to cheer
The Pilgrim child whose wasting face
   Was meekly turned to hear;
And drew his toil-worn sleeve across,
   To brush the manly tear
From cheeks that never changed in woe,
   And never blanched in fear.

The weary Pilgrim slumbers,
   His resting-place unknown;
His hands were crossed, his lids were closed,
   The dust was o'er him strewn.

The drifting soil, the moldering leaf,
   Along the sod were blown,
His mound has melted into earth,
   His memory lives alone.

So let it live unfading,
   The memory of the dead,
Long as the pale anemone
   Springs where their tears were shed,
Or raining in the summer's wind,
   In flakes of burning red,
The wild rose sprinkles with its leaves
   The turf where once they bled!

Yea, when the frowning bulwarks
   That guard this holy strand
Have sunk beneath the trampling surge
   In beds of sparkling sand,
While in the waste of ocean
   One hoary rock shall stand,
Be this its latest legend:
   HERE WAS THE PILGRIM'S LAND.
          — Oliver Wendell Holmes.

HYMN FOR 22D DECEMBER.

Tune: *Lyons.*

A ROCK in the wilderness welcomed our
  sires,
From bondage far over the dark rolling sea ;
On that holy altar they kindled the fires,
  Jehovah, which glow in our bosoms for thee !

Thy blessings descended in sunshine and shower,
  Or rose from the soil that was sown by thy
    hand ;
The mountain and valley rejoiced in thy power,
  And heaven encircled and smiled on the land.

The Pilgrims of old an example have given
  Of mild resignation, devotion, and love,
Which beams like the star in the blue vault of
    heaven,
  A beacon-light hung in the mansions above.

In church and cathedral we kneel in our prayer,
  Their temple and chapel were valley and hill ;
But God is the same in the aisle or the air,
  And he is the Rock that we lean upon still.

— Author Unknown.

BURIAL HILL.[1]

A H ! then all tenderly we thought,
  We thought with pride and wonder,
How — Freedom's price divinely taught —
  They stood unflinching yonder ;

Though wintry chillness reigned around,
  And wintry winds were howling,
Though only savage man was found,
  And savage beasts were prowling.

Anew we felt their hopes and fears,
  When want and sickness wasted ;
As through the lingering weary years,
  Of sorrow's cup they tasted.

Grand souls ! that with heroic will
  The waves of trouble breasted ;
Not e'en did women falter, till
  Beneath that turf they rested.

For God, for truth, for man, they bore
  Loss, exile, grief, and danger ;
As Christ, the Lord they loved, of yore
  Accepted earth's low manger.

[1] A portion of a longer poem. 1865.

And there above their sacred dust
　Whose names shall never perish,
We vowed *their faith*, a holy trust
　For all mankind, to cherish.

O God, who heard'st our prayer and song
　'Neath heaven's high dome ascending,
Bid us in thine own might be strong,
　For that pure faith contending.

　　.　　.　　.　　.　　.　　.　　.　　.

Oh, wake, ye sons of Pilgrim sires !
　Go, live in power and beauty
The life sublime their faith inspires ;
　Its watchword — GOD AND DUTY !
　　　　　　　　　　— *Ray Palmer.*

THE MAYFLOWER.

SAD Mayflower ! watched by winter stars
　And nursed by winter gales,
With petals of the sleeted spars,
　And leaves of frozen sails !

What had she in those dreary hours,
　　Within her ice-rimmed bay,
In common with the wildwood flowers,
　　The first sweet smiles of May?

Yet " God be praised ! " the Pilgrim said,
　　Who saw the blossoms peer
Above the brown leaves, dry and dead,
　　" Behold our Mayflower here ! "

" God wills it, here our rest shall be,
　　Our years of wandering o'er,
For us the Mayflower of the sea
　　Shall spread her sails no more."

O sacred flowers of faith and hope,
　　As sweetly now as then
Ye bloom on many a birchen slope,
　　In many a pine-dark glen.

Behind the sea-wall's rugged length,
　　Unchanged, your leaves unfold
Like love behind the manly strength
　　Of the brave hearts of old.

So live the fathers in their sons,
　　Their sturdy faith be ours,
And ours the love that overruns
　　Its rocky strength with flowers.

The Pilgrims' wild and wintry day
 Its shadow round us draws ;
The Mayflower of his stormy bay,
 Our Freedom's struggling cause.

But warmer suns erelong shall bring
 To life the frozen sod ;
And, through dead leaves of hope, shall
  spring
Afresh the flowers of God !
      — *John G. Whittier.*

FAST DAY SPORT.

(A.D. 1648.)

SHAME, shame upon ye, godless lads,
 To take your matchlocks down,
And to the forest hie for game,
 When all the folk in town
Were gathered in the meeting-house,
 In Sabbath garb arrayed,
To fast and pray this solemn day,
 As Governor Winthrop bade !

Ye think, perchance, I failed to mark
  Some empty places there ;
Nay, nay, I do my duty, lads,
  Though ye may mock and stare.
I ween, despite your many smirks,
  When all is said and done,
Ye 'll think the hare ye dangle there
  Was hardly worth the fun.

I 've copied fair your names, young sirs,
  Trespass, — one shilling nine, —
And governor's grandsons though ye be,
  I wot ye 'll pay the fine ;
It should be doubled for the sin
  Of such example set ;
I 'm sorely sad a Boston lad
  So strangely could forget.

Ye did not? ha! the bold offence
  Was a deliberate one?
Ye meant to scout the Fast day, when
  Ye went with dog and gun?
Out on such worldly lawlessness !
  Ye well deserve to be
Left in the lurch with king and church
  In Suffolk by the sea !

It ought to make the crimson shame
　Your braggart faces flood,
When ye remember that your veins
　Are warm with Winthrop blood!
Now had ye been Sir Harry's chicks,
　To do and dare with such
Pert looks as send my hair on end,
　I had not cared so much.

But Governor Winthrop's grandsons! heigh!
　How godless folk will prate!
He can not make his household keep
　The Fast day of the state!
Nay, do I hear aright? ye say
　He gave ye leave to go
To-day and track (alack! alack!)
　The rabbits through the snow?

Ye look so roguish, scarce I think
　Ye mean the word ye spake;
But since ye 've dared with bold affront
　The righteous law to break,
Though even the governor's self forgot
　His bounden duty, mine
Is clear; ye 'll pay this very day
　Each farthing of your fine.
　　　　　　　— Margaret J. Preston.

THE PURITAN MAIDEN'S MAY-DAY.

(A.D. 1686.)

AH, well-a-day! the grandams say
    That they had merry times
When they were young, and gayly rung
    The May-day morning chimes.

Before the dark was gone, the lark
    Had left her grassy nest,
And, soaring high, set all the sky
    Athrob from East to West!

The hawthorn bloom with rich perfume
    Was whitening English lanes,
The dewy air was every-where
    Alive with May-day strains;

And laughing girls with tangled curls,
    And eyes that gleamed and glanced,
And ruddy boys with mirth and noise
    Around the May-pole danced.

Ah me! the sight of such delight,
    The joy, the whirl, the din,
Such merriment, such glad content —
    How could it be a sin?

When children crowned the May-pole round
  With daisies from the sod,
What was it, pray, but their child's way
  Of giving thanks to God?

The wild bee sups from buttercups
  The honey at the brim;
May I not take their buds and make
  A posy up for him?

If, as I pass knee-deep through grass
  This May-day cool and bright,
And see away on Boston Bay
  The lines of shimmering light,

I gather there great bunches fair
  Of mayflower as I roam,
And with them round my forehead crowned,
  Go ladened with them home;

And then, if Bess and I should dress
  A May-pole with our wreath,
And just for play, this holiday,
  Should dare to dance beneath,

My father's brow would frown enow:
  " Child! why hast thou a mind
For popish days and Romish ways,
  And lusts we 've left behind?"

Our grandam says that her May-days,
  With mirth and song and flowers,
And lilt of rhymes and village chimes,
  Were happier far than ours.

If, as I ween, upon the green
  She danced with merry din,
Yet lived to be the saint I see,
  How can I count it sin?
                      — *Margaret J. Preston.*

FOREFATHERS' DAY.[1]

THE wandering sun, ranging through south-
    ern skies,
Has touched his wintry solstice. O'er the north
Fall the chill shadows, and the sickly days,
Pale-faced and wan, are quickly lost in night.
From the cold heavens, through lonely midnight
    hours,
The glittering stars look down on fields of ice,
On plains and mountains wrapped in robes of
    snow.

[1] Read at Boston Congregational Club Festival, December, 1880.

Along the headlands of our rock-bound coast
The wild waves roll, and the hoarse murmurs
    break,
Telling the lonely dwellers by the sea
Of far-off winds and storms and tossing barks.
Now is the midnight of our northern year.
Nature has laid aside her flowery robes,
And clothed herself in soberest attire.
All sights and sounds, in earth and air and
    heaven,
Recall those stern historic days of old
When our brave Pilgrim sires, battling with
    waves,
Struggling with icy winds and adverse fate,
Made their rude entry on these western shores.
Now, in our well-filled homes, by genial fires,
We read the tale, — tell o'er the honored names,
Those grand and simple names that can not die,
And proudly trace our ancient lineage.

We read the critics too, those sharp-eyed men,
Who search all precious ointments through and
    through,
Not for the ointment's sake, to prove its worth,
But, if so be, to find out and report
Some smallest fly that may have lodged therein.

Our Pilgrim critics are an ancient brood,
Hovering about the rock from age to age,
With nods portentous and with croaking voice.
'T is well to read these critics, well to know
Their inmost thought, and follow where they
    lead.
Guided by them and walking in their light,
Let us now re-construct our Pilgrim sires,
And show what men our fathers should have
    been.

The Pilgrim Father should have been a man
    Who had no private prejudice to smother,
Built on a large, expansive, liberal plan,
    To whom one thing were good as any other ;
Who, had he lived, back when the race began,
    Would not have minded when Cain killed his
        brother ;
A man so very round and full and pious
As to be free from every shade of bias.

He should have patronized with equal zeal
    Every adventurous and random rover ;
Have freely shared his dear-bought common weal
    With every renegade that might come over ;

Ready to grant each wanderer's appeal,
  Whether he came from Holland, Dublin,
    Dover;
A man who held it strict impartiality
Not to distinguish virtue from rascality.

Once here, our Pilgrim's first and foremost thought
  Ought to have been to please his Indian neigh-
    bor;
What though the cunning, lazy savage sought
  To gain his living without care or labor;
Still, our good Pilgrim ought not to have
    brought
  To this new world his musket and his saber;
It surely was not generous and good
To frighten these poor children of the wood.

They were the dwellers on this western soil
  Centuries before the Mayflower went a-cruis-
    ing;
If they preferred to live exempt from toil,
  Who had the right to hinder them from choos-
    ing?
Or, if they forced their wives to slave and moil,
  Beating or killing any one refusing,
The Pilgrim Father was a stranger here,
What arrogance in him to interfere!

He should have landed on this western shore
    With less of Bible, and with more of science ;
Bible is good, but had he pondered o'er
    What science taught, and made that his reli-
        ance,
He could have reared, from his exhaustless store,
    An empire grand, to bid the world defiance ;
Great pity that with chances so prodigious
He should have been a trifle too religious.

Given, just scientific lore enough
    Simply to analyze that famous bowlder
Called Plymouth Rock, where " breaking waves
        dashed " — rough —
    That rock which thrills with awe each new
        beholder ;
Given, the mica, quartz, and other stuff
    Employed and used by the primeval molder
To forge, by aid of underground caloric,
That marvelous rock now grown to be historic ;

Given, the power to tell, like modern sages,
    Somewhere   within   five   hundred   thousand
        years
How old that bowlder is, and what the stages
    By which it journeyed to these Plymouth piers,

To trace its starting-point in by-gone ages,
    And show how easy every thing appears, —
Items like these are solid information,
Well fitted to build up a mighty nation.

But we go prating on about this rock,
    Its mental, moral, and religious uses ;
We treat it like some huge æsthetic block,
    Whose very name to boundless good conduces :
We feel a kind of sentimental shock
    When any scoffer offers his abuses :
From sixteen hundred twenty to this day,
The rock has served in this peculiar way.

Here endeth the first lesson.   Turn the page
    And we may find all freshly spread before us
The counter-charges of a later age,
    Which may, by contrast, comfort and restore us;
Critics in war with critics will engage
    Long as the centuries go rolling o'er us :
If we could tarry till their strife were ended,
Our Pilgrim sires would surely be defended.

These counter-charges which we have in hand
    Seem, in their contrasts, just a little funny.
The Pilgrims, now, are not a pious band ;
    They came, it seems, intent on making money.

They fancied that this rough New England land
  Might prove to them a land of milk and
    honey;
And so they ventured o'er a stormy ocean
To pay at Mammon's shrine their pure devotion.

They were a wandering clan that could not rest
  Or live contented in their own condition;
And when they left their ancient English nest,
  They only showed their restless disposition;
Ready to journey east or journey west
  Upon their money-making expedition,
They tried old Holland, and, ignobly failing,
Away to Plymouth Rock they went a-sailing.

But know ye well, O critics, ye spend your
    strength for nought;
All harmless fall the weapons your cunning
    hands have wrought;
The men ye seek to injure have reached a height
    sublime,
Whereon they sit secure against the accidents
    of time:
The rolling years have tried them, the centuries
    have passed,
And clothed them with a glory that shall forever
    last.

The wandering birds that fly afar are wise to
    know their hour ;
Seeking the fields of upper air and thwarting
    human power,
They voyage on unguided by compass or by
    chart
Along these clear and azure heights, safe from
    the hunter's dart ;
A law they know not moves them straight to
    their distant nest,
Unerringly they journey and find their promised
    rest.

So the old patriarchs journeyed, moved by the
    call of God,
Earth's wanderers, unknowing the pathway
    which they trod :
And so the Pilgrims journeyed, leaving their
    native land,
Going they knew not whither by some divine
    command ;
With faith and loving patience they trod their
    weary way,
And so their names stand glorified before our
    eyes to-day.

The best and purest wisdom is wisdom of the
    heart
Untouched by human cunning, unstained by
    earthly art ;
He that by craft will save his life shall lose it
    at the end ;
He that will lose his life shall find an everlasting
    friend :
God has his chosen children, his favorites on
    the earth,
Raised out of toil and sorrow by an immortal
    birth.

               — Increase N. Tarbox.

THE PILGRIMS.

ONCE a handful, brave and daring
    As young eagles from their nest,
Sought for human right and freedom
    Over ocean's foaming crest.

Giving friendship, love, and kindred.
    All the sacred worth of tears,
Giving God their faith as treasure,
    Stored for all the coming years.

"God and Freedom," was the watchword
    Of that noble Pilgrim band,
And God led them to that freedom
    By his own almighty hand.

Rocked by cold winds, lashed by billows,
    Plunging where the white waves scethe,
He who rules the tempest guides them,
    His strong arm is underneath.

O'er that ship an angel hovered
    As the stormy voyage ran ;
Caught the tears of suffering woman,
    Heard the sighs of suffering man.

Round that ship a glory lingers,
    Sailing on from year to year ;
Round its masts bright rainbows circle,
    Caught from every sacred tear.

Not the Rock alone is holy,
    Where their chrismal prayer was made,
For the hand of God, in blessing,
    Over all the land was laid.

Though the Pilgrim Fathers slumber,
    Still their spirits are not dead ;
Far beyond the inland rivers
    Now their children's children tread.

Now a nation calls them blessed,
  For the freedom which they bought,
And the world has been made better
  For their lesson, nobly taught.

Hope, O Christian, through all trials ;
  Through life's tempests on the way ;
Hearts will bless you on the morrow,
  For your triumphs yesterday.

Like the sword of Standish, bearing
  Only God's grand message, " Peace,"
Spreading love among the nations
  Until wars and tumults cease.

                    — *Sylvia Brown.*

MEMORY OF OUR FATHERS.

IN pleasant lands have fallen the lines
    That bound our goodly heritage,
And safe beneath our sheltering vines
    Our youth is blest, and soothed our age.

What thanks, O God, to thee are due,
  That thou didst plant our fathers here ;
And watch and guard them as they grew,
  A vineyard to the Planter dear.

The toils they bore our ease have wrought;
They sowed in tears — in joy we reap;
The birthright they so dearly bought
We 'll guard, till we with them shall sleep.

Thy kindness to our fathers shown
In weal and woe through all the past,
Their grateful sons, O God, shall own,
While here their name and race shall last.

— Flint.

THE MAYFLOWER ON NEW ENG-LAND'S COAST.

THE Mayflower on New England's coast has
furled her tattered sail,
And through her chafed and moaning shrouds
December's breezes wail;
Yet on their icy deck behold a meek but daunt-
less band,
Who, for the right to worship God, have left
their native land;
And to this dreary wilderness this glorious boon
they bring —
*A church without a bishop, and a state without a
king!*

Those daring men, those gentle wives, say,
    wherefore do they come?
Why rend they all the tender ties of kindred
    and of home?
'T is heaven assigns their noble work, man's
    spirit to unbind :
They come not for themselves alone, they come
    for all mankind ;
And to the empire of the West this glorious
    boon they bring —
A church without a bishop, and a state without a
    king !

Then prince and prelate, hope no more to bend
    them to your sway ;
Devotion's fire inflames their breasts while free-
    dom points their way ;
And in their brave heart's estimate, 't were bet-
    ter not to be
Than quail beneath a despot where the soul
    can not be free ;
And therefore o'er a wintry wave those exiles
    come to bring
A church without a bishop, and a state without a
    king !

And still their spirit, in their sons, with freedom
  walks abroad ;
The Bible is our only creed, our only sovereign,
  God !
- The hand is raised, the word is spoke, the joyful
  pledge is given,
And boldly on our banner floats, in the free air
  of heaven,
That motto of our sainted sires, and loud we 'll
  make it ring :
A church without a bishop, and a state without a
  king !

— Charles Hall.

MEMORIAL HYMN.[1]

FIRM as the rock beneath their feet,
    The saintly Pilgrims stood ;
On thee, O God, their trust was stayed,
Thy voice their steadfast souls obeyed,
And thou didst answer when they prayed
    Beside the wintry flood ;
Didst give them strength in faith sublime
To work the noblest work of time !

[1] Written for, and sung at, the memorial celebration in Boston, 21 December, 1870.

To-day by centuries we count
  The slowly measured years ;
And lo ! wide o'er a smiling land
Fair homes and sacred temples stand ;
Where frowned rude wastes and forests grand,
  A peopled realm appears ;
O'er hills and plains, from sea to sea,
Sweep thronging millions of the free !

Tears for the days of deadly strife ;
  Tears for the young and brave,
Who, fired by freedom's battle-cry,
Flung broad her banner to the sky,
Content on gory fields to lie,
  That they her home might save ;
That chains from every hand might fall,
And love's wide arms encircle all !

As thou didst hear, O faithful God,
  The prayer our fathers said,
So hear us while, like them, to thee
We for our children bend the knee ;
Let them to distant ages be
  As if the Pilgrims, dead,
In them did wake and live again ;
Their shields the shields of mighty men !

O Christ! be thine the Pilgrims' land!
  Reign thou from shore to shore;
Here let thy Church, beneath thy sway,
Grow fairer till her bridal day,
When thou shalt come in glad array —
  Her Lord — as mountains o'er,
In splendor robed, the morning sun
Ascends his flaming course to run!

Praise God! praise him who changeth not!
  Our fathers' God and ours;
To thee our thankful praise we bring,
Ancient of days! Our glorious king!
Let earth and heaven together sing
  With all their raptured powers,
Till listening stars shall catch the strain,
And shout the chorus back again!

— Ray Palmer.

FOREFATHERS' DAY.[1]

ALMIGHTY God! to thee we raise
  Our hymn of thankfulness and praise,
Within the hollow of whose hand
The Pilgrim sought his promised land!

[1] For the celebration of 1882.

Not the rich pastures of the vine,
Flowing with honey, milk, and wine,
But bleak shores sought by storm and sea,
Their rude, sole welcome — *Thou art free!*

With corn he wooed the sullen soil,
But more with learning, home, and toil ;
Till now no vineyard of the sun
Blooms like the wilderness he won.

Inspired by faith, in purpose great,
He steadfast set his Church and State,
Made them to stand 'gainst flood and shock,
For both he built upon the rock.

One taught — to God and conscience true —
More light to seek the right to do ;
The other broadened to the span
Of man's equality with man.

Children of fathers such as he,
Be ours the true nobility !
Lords of the realm, they served its growth ;
To serve be still the freeman's oath.

— John D. Long.

HYMN FOR 21 DECEMBER, 1870.

GREAT God of all! in humble, grateful
    prayer
We come before thee now on bended knee,
And thank thee that thou didst our fathers spare
    From the wild dangers of a wintry sea.

We thank thee that, when dangers greater far
    Encompassed them, that brave hearts might
        appall,
Thou didst support them, and didst let the star
    Of hope shine on their hearts and strengthen
        all.

And we, their children, on this joyous day,
    No longer peril-driven or tempest-tossed,
Approach thy throne in thankfulness, and pray
    Our fathers' bright examples be not lost.

May we, like them, have strength and courage
    given,
Bear bravely up e'en though we feel the rod ;
Know that a life well spent leads on to heaven,
    And *duties'* paths are but the paths to God.
                — *Nathaniel Spooner.*

HYMN.[1]

TO Thee, O God! whose guiding hand
   Our fathers led across the sea,
And brought them to this barren shore,
   Where they might freely worship thee;

To thee, O God! whose arm sustained
   Their footsteps in this desert land,
Where sickness lurked and death assailed,
   And foes beset on every hand;

To thee, O God! we lift our eyes;
   To thee our grateful voices raise,
And, kneeling at thy gracious throne,
   Devoutly join in hymns of praise.

Our fathers' God! incline thine ear,
   And listen to our heartfelt prayer;
Surround us with thy heavenly grace,
   And guard us with thy constant care.

Our fathers' God! in thee we 'll trust;
   Sheltered by thee from every harm,
We 'll follow where thy hand shall guide,
   And lean on thy sustaining arm.

              — *William T. Davis.*

[1] Sung at Plymouth at the 250th anniversary, 21 December, 1870.

DEDICATION OF HITCHCOCK LIBRARY.

(December 21, 1874.)

I.

GOD of our Pilgrim sires, to thee
　　All might and majesty belong ;
Before thy face we bow the knee,
　　And lift aloud our grateful song.

By thy strong arm the Pilgrim band
　　Were kept in all their stormy way
Until they trod this goodly land
　　And gave to us this happy day.

We bring our gift before thy throne,
　　This labor which our hands have wrought,
And consecrate to thee alone
　　This treasure-house of sacred thought.

Choicer than gold though thrice refined,
　　Or all the gems that ocean rolls,
Are these fair riches of the mind,
　　This garnered wealth of holy souls.

God of our sires, still let that grace,
　　That strength, which made the fathers bold
Descend upon the Pilgrim race,
　　As coming years shall be unrolled.

II.

We sing our gladsome hymn of praise,
   And bless our fathers' God,
While we recount the former days,
   And trace the pathway trod.

How many hearts this hope has filled,
   The living and the dead!
How many hands have wrought to build
   This temple where we tread!

But one our warmest praise demands,
   His gift we here recall,
By whom this finished structure stands,
   Whose name adorns our hall.

He gave, and passed from earth away
   To his unseen employ
E'er he could see this crowning day,
   Or share our festive joy.

But here, embalmed, his gift shall last,
   His substance shall endure;
And as the rolling years go past,
   His heritage is sure.
               — *Increase N. Tarbox.*

THE BOYS' REDOUBT.

(October, 1775.)

IN continental buff-and-blue,
　With lappets richly laced,
Beneath the shade the elm-trees made,
　A martial figure paced.

Along the sluggish Charles's banks
　He bent at length his way,
Just as the gun, at set of sun,
　Went booming o'er the bay.

His soul was racked with doubt and strife,
　Despondence gloomed his eye ;
He needs must bear his weight of care
　Out to the open sky.

The breeze that flapped his soldier's cloak,
　The woods so broad and dim,
The tides whose sway no bonds could stay,
　All seemed so free to him !

Yet the young nation that had wrung,
　Beyond the angry seas,
From savage grace a refuge-place
　To pray as they might please,

Must it be hounded from its haunts?
   Be fettered at the stake?
Be forced again to wear the chain
   It risked its all to break?

His step grew heavier with the thought,
   His lips less firm were set;
It could not be that such as he
   Must yield! and yet — and yet —

How could they even hope to win
   A single fight in lack
Of every thing, while England's king
   Had Europe at his back?

Thus musing sad beside the Charles,
   He saw the Cambridge boys,
An eager band, pile up the sand
   With roar of riot noise.

" Ha! lads, what do you here?" he said,
   Arrested by their shout.
" What do we here? why, give us cheer;
   We 're building a redoubt!

" Who knows how soon Lord Howe may come,
   And all his lion cubs,
With growls and snarls, straight up the Charles,
   In his old British tubs?

" And creeping from them in the dark,
    As quiet as a mouse,
  Now what if they should snatch away,
    Right out of Vassal House

" Our new-made chief, before a man
    Has leave to fire a gun?
  That ends it! for there 'll be no war
    Without a Washington!

" Our fathers' hands are filled with work;
    Besides, they 're grieving still
  For Warren and the gallant band
    That fell at Bunker Hill.

" So we will help them as we can;
    You wear the buff-and-blue;
  Yet we aver that we 're ready, sir,
    To fight as well as you.

" May be you 're on the general's staff;
    Then say we Cambridge boys
  Will yell and shout from our redoubt
    With such a savage noise

" That all the vessels in the bay
    Will hear the wild uproar
  And swear again that Prescott's men
    Are lining all the shore! "

" Brave lads ! " the soldier said, and raised
    The cap that hid his brow ;
" Some day, some day, I 'll surely pay
    The debt I owe you now !

" Your high, heroic, mettled hearts,
    Your faith that wavers not,
To me are more than cannon's store,
    Or tons of shell and shot.

" What people ever fails to gain
    The patriot's dearest prize,
When ' die or win ' is blazing in
    The very children's eyes?

" No need to bear the general word
    Of tasks so rich in cheer ;
He makes his due salute to you —
    You see the General here ! "

          — *Margaret J. Preston.*

FOREFATHERS' DAY.

ON this low rock beside the bay,
    With lonely woods and waters round,
The steps once heard at break of day
    Fill every village with their sound.

Again we tell how great the deed
  Of those who here their journey stayed,
And, building cabins for their need,
  Foundations of an empire laid.

We see again, to these wild shores,
  Their vessel sail the path of light,
And hail the morning's golden floors
  Above the winter and the night.

In God their dwelling-place they made ;
  They toiled supremely him to please ;
So, ever in their toil they prayed,
  And built this nation on their knees.

—*Albert Bryant.*

THE SPIRIT OF FOREFATHERS' DAY.

FAITH ROBINSON.

THEY called her Faith, this winsome baby
    girl,
With soft blue eyes and cheek of rose and pearl,
Born in old Holland, where the Pilgrims stayed
Until the Mayflower frail her anchor weighed
For the strange country far across the sea,
Where faith in God taught them their home
    should be.

" Faith is a comfort, both in word and deed,
A gift from heaven ; " in this they all agreed.
" Whether on sea or land, she has the grace
Of golden sunshine in a gloomy place."

The years flew by, and Faith grew brave and tall,
A comfort still was this sweet maid to all.
Whate'er perplexed them she was wont to say :
" The Bible tells us in such times to pray."

One year no rain fell. All the fields were dry.
" The corn and grass and sheep will surely die,
And when the winter comes, ah, sorry day ! "
" Why, grandsire dear, the people all must pray.

" I 'll call them now, from house to house I 'll go ;
They 'll come, I'm sure, if we but let them know
At four o'clock, on Deacon Fuller's hill,
We 'll pray for rain enough to turn the mill ;
For some there are now almost out of bread."
These were the words the little maiden said.

The people came ; the sky was hot and clear,
No breath of rain nor sign of cloud was near ;
They climbed the hill with faces worn and sad :
Faith followed singing like a birdling glad.
To her granddame and mother straight she came.

"I went," said she, "to fetch these for the
　　rain," —
She'd brought a cloak, and blankets two had
　　she, —
"These are for you, the cloak will cover me."

"Faith *is* a comfort!" all the women said.
"*Such* faith!" the elder sighed and bowed his
　　head.
The people lingered long upon their knees
With prayers and sobs.　A shiver stirred the trees,
The air grew cool, the sun was clouded in.
"The want of faith in us is deadly sin,"
The deacon said.　"Let us not err again!"
Then patter, patter came the welcome rain.

That was the spirit of Forefathers' Day.
"Give it to us," let all the children pray;
"Lord, give us faith and keep us pure and
　　strong,
Help us to serve the right, to right the wrong.
Oh, make us worthy of those Pilgrim sires
Who prayed for us about their first camp-fires,
While wintry skies bent o'er them cold and gray."
In faith they prayed — that made Forefathers'
　　Day.

　　　　　　　　　　　　— *Annie A. Preston.*

OUR FATHERS.

WE own that guiding hand,
 Which, in the years of old,
Led to this chosen land
 Our fathers, firm and bold,
Brought them across the stormy sea,
To build this empire of the free.

They came with faith in God,
 They came with faith in man;
On this fresh virgin sod
 To try their untried plan;
To give this realm of freedom birth
And shed new light around the earth.

Soon as our godly sires
 These new-found shores had trod,
They lit their altar-fires
 And claimed the land for God;
They filled the forest shades with light,
And turned to day the savage night.

    — *Increase N. Tarbox.*

FOREFATHERS' DAY, 1883.

THE EVERLASTING REMEMBRANCE.

WHY die ye not? Ye men of God,
 Ye women saintly, who beside
Husband and brother fearless trod
Where Plymouth Rock the sea defied!
Where'er I turn my eyes, behold
Change ruleth all things; dull decay
Treads on the heels of life; and cold
In the still tomb forever laid,
The best and loveliest of to-day.
The noblest in God's image made,
To-morrow straight have passed away!
Where Art has reared her massive towers
Storied with names renowned of yore,
Crumbled by Time's slow-wasting powers,
Lie heaps of moss-grown ruins hoar;
And Thebes and Athens all too well
The tale of perished grandeurs tell.
Warriors of might and monarchs proud,
Before whom trembling nations bowed,
Whose dust grand mausoleums keep,
In dark oblivion silent sleep,
Yet live ye on; your praises found
On reverent lips the world around.

So, as in thoughtful mood I stood
Where Burial Hill o'erlooks the tide,
Came visions of the great and good
Who bravely lived and nobly died ;
Who, dauntless, to this lonely strand
God's holy ark of freedom bore ;
Self-exiled from that motherland
Whose shores their eyes should greet no more,
Firm as the rock on which they trod,
In faith sublime and purpose high,
For unborn ages and for God,
They dared to suffer and to die.

Beneath thy turf, O sacred hill,
Their canopy the changeful sky,
They sleep while years their circuits fill,
And the slow centuries go by ;
Nor mind they wintry tempests more,
Nor heed the angry ocean's roar ;
But ever o'er that peaceful sleep
Their faithful watch the angels keep.

Illustrious band ! whose future then
In God's deep counsels hidden lay,
Ye faltered not, but followed, when
Through deepest darkness led the way ;

A way of anguish though it seemed,
Yet, heaven inspired, ye hoped ; and dreamed
That on, beyond that dismal gloom,
Should rise at last a joyous morn,
When the waste wilderness should bloom,
And children's children, freemen born,
Should throng in countless millions o'er
The vast expanse from shore to shore ;
When, for the savage yell and knife,
Should come just laws and cultured life ;
And cities rise with spire and dome,
The marts of commerce and the home
Of men whom loftiest thoughts inspire,
Born of religion's heavenly fire ;
Where none would quench the sacred flame
Of freedom, none consent to bear,
On mind or hand enchained, the shame
Which only the debased can wear.

Oh ! if from these calm skies to-day,
The mighty voice of God should say :
" Ye sleepers, wake !   To life arise,
Ye great in soul !   Ye nobly good !
Stand up as when of old ye stood,
And with clear vision lift your eyes ! "

As ye again to life should start,
The same in mind, in thought, in heart,
As when, o'erborne with ills, ye gave
Your wasted bodies to the grave ;
Ah ! on those eyes at once awake
From death's long sleep, what wonders break !
Behold what then ye dreamed ! Ye wept
With sickness, care and sorrow worn,
With hopes and fears alternate torn,
As near yon Rock your watch ye kept.
To-day, as here ye stand, once more
Before you the same surf-beat shore,
Above you the same heavens and sun
Which saw your glorious work begun ;
Ye look, — O bliss without alloy, —
Ye weep again, but now *for joy!*

The griefs that in your Pilgrim years
Wrung from the bravest many a sigh ;
That wet uplifted eyes with tears,
When none could help save God on high,
Seem troubled visions of the night
That vanished with the morning light.
Beyond your dreams, your hopes, your thought,
Lo ! what God's faithful love hath wrought !

Before your raptured eyes ye see
A refuge for the world's opprest ;
A noble empire strong and free,
Where the poor exile finds his rest ;
Land of all lands most richly blest !

Ye can not die !   Around your names
The splendor of true glory flames ;
That glory, matchless and sublime,
Not bought with blood, not stained with crime,
O'er the wide world its radiance throws,
And, all undimmed by change or time,
On through the ages brighter glows !
As from fresh beds of flowers at morn
Perfumes are breathed that fill the air ;
That on the genial breezes borne,
Bear grateful sweetness every-where,
So from this soil ye wet with tears,
Where wrestled faith through lingering years,
Forces divine have silent sprung,
Whose influence, like sweet odors flung
O'er distant realms, hath kindly wrought,
Hath quickened life and hope and thought,
Made glad humanity, and broke
Cold tyranny's dread, hateful yoke,

With truths by God's own wisdom taught.
  Goodness and truth, with God allied,
As his eternal throne abide !
The glory won by guilt shall fade ;
  Its proud memorials turn to dust ;
But fresh, immortal, undecayed,
Shall live the *glory of the just!*
— *Ray Palmer.*

FOREFATHERS' DAY.

PORTUGUESE HYMN.

OH, strong is our God in the might of his
  sway,
He speaks, and the seas and the tempests obey ;
He guides the frail bark on its perilous path,
And holds back the surges that break in their
  wrath.

Oh, strong is our God, for he casteth down
  kings,
But broods o'er the humble with sheltering
  wings ;
He shames and dishonors the pride of the
  throne,
But lifts up the lowly and makes them his own.

Oh, strong is our God, for this realm of the west
He guarded and kept for a refuge and rest,
He gave to our fathers these fountains and rills,
The wealth of the valleys and strength of the
    hills.

Oh, strong is our God, and what song shall
    unfold
The wonders he wrought for our fathers of old?
Through sorrow and gladness, in sunshine and
    storm,
Their faith still beheld his invisible form.

Oh, strong is our God, and the nations are
    strong
That bow in his temples with worship and song;
The fear of the Lord is the strength of the state,
And blest are the men at his altars who wait.

—— *Increase N. Tarbox.*

THE PILGRIM FOREFATHERS.

'NEATH hoary moss on crumbling stones
        Their names are fading day by day;
The fashions of their lives and speech
    From sight and sound have passed away.

The shores they found so bleak, so bare,
    Shine now with riches gay and proud ;
And we, light-hearted, dance on ground
    Where they in anguish wept and bowed.

Unto the faith they bought so dear,
    We pay each day less reverent heed ;
And boast, perhaps, that we outgrow
    The narrowness which marked their creed.

A shallow boast of thankless hearts,
    In evil generation born ;
By side of those old Pilgrim men
    The ages shall hold us in scorn.

Find me the men on earth who care
    Enough for faith or creed to-day,
To seek a barren wilderness
    For simple liberty to pray ;

Men who for simple sake of God
    All titles, riches, would refuse,
And in their stead, disgrace and shame
    And bitter poverty would choose.

We find them not. Alas ! the age,
    In all its light, hath blinder grown ;
In all its plenty, starves because
    It seeks to live by bread alone.

We owe them all we have of good :
　Our sunny skies, our fertile fields ;
Our freedom, which to all oppressed
　A continent of refuge yields.

And what we have of ill, of shame,
　Our broken word, our greed for gold,
Our reckless schemes and treacheries,
　In which men's souls are bought and sold, —

All these have come because we left
　The paths that these forefathers trod ;
The simple, single-hearted ways
　In which they feared and worshiped God.

Despise their name and creed who will !
　Pity their poverty who dare !
Their lives knew joys, their lives wore crowns
　We do not know, we can not wear.

And if so be that it is saved,
　Our poor republic, stained and bruised,
'T will be because we lay again
　Their corner-stones which we refused.

　　　　　　　　— H. H.

DECEMBER 21st, 1620–1870.

YE children of New England,
Wherever ye may be,
Whether ye keep the ancient homes
Down by the ancient sea ;
Treading the rocky pathways
Your fathers trod before,
Hearing the wild Atlantic break
Along her stormy shore ;
Or if afar ye wander
O'er the prairies of the west,
Or down the wide Pacific slopes,
Your weary footsteps rest :

Come, listen to my story,
The grand ancestral lay,
Which, as the world grows older,
Grows newer every day ;
Which touches men with pity,
And touches men with pride,
In the memory of those noble souls,
For God who lived and died.

This is no play of fancy
  To catch a listless ear ;
No strange and shadowy legend
  For idle minds to hear ;
No tale of love and sorrow
  To rob the eye of sleep,
O'er which pale sickly maidens
  May weep and read and weep.

'T is a tale of faith and patience,
  And a tale of cruel wrong,
When the good to earth were trampled
  By the haughty and the strong ;
The brave, heroic Pilgrims
  Could find no place of rest
Save o'er the stormy ocean,
  In the forests of the west.

Behold these storm-tost Pilgrims
  On a rough and barren shore ;
With the sounding sea behind them,
  And the wilderness before ;
Hungry and cold they house them
  In their dwellings rude and low,
While the night winds howl around them
  With their drifting clouds of snow.

In these nights of care and watching,
　Long nights unblest with sleep,
What strange, fantastic terrors
　Over the spirits creep !
Out from these unknown forests
　Come stealing on the ear,
Weird and mysterious voices,
　That chill the soul with fear.

Oh, the terrors of that winter,
　When men sickened day by day,
And one by one, as weeks rolled on,
　They dropped and passed away !
There was no harsh and murmuring voice,
　No sad, complaining cry,
But silently they heard the call
　And laid them down to die.

Meekly as to the slaughter
　The patient lamb is led,
Meekly before the shearers
　As the sheep bows down her head,
So bowed these humble Pilgrims
　Before the chastening rod,
And opened not their mouth to doubt
　The goodness of their God.

Strong men and gentle women,
   The maiden in her bloom,
The little child, the gray-haired sire,
   Slept in their hill-side tomb;
They were buried there in darkness,
   And the living smoothed their bed,
That the fierce savage might not tell
   The number of the dead.

And when the genial sun came back,
   And these dark months were o'er,
When through the budding forests
   The soft winds blew once more,
Half of their number could not feel
   Its sweet reviving breath, —
They slept upon the burial hill
   The icy sleep of death.

But these days of fiery trial,
   Of scorn and hate, are o'er,
And now these grand old Pilgrim sires
   Shall live to die no more;
Men kindle at their virtues,
   They tell with swelling pride
The story of those men of old,
   For God who lived and died.

And as the years roll onward,
  Through the ages yet to be,
As wider grows and wider
  This empire of the free,
Grander shall grow the story
  Of those men, true and tried,
Those noble and heroic souls,
  For God who lived and died.
                    — *Increase N. Tarbox.*

ELDER FAUNCE AT PLYMOUTH ROCK.

AN old, old man!
    His hair is white as snow,
His feeble footsteps slow,
And the light of his eyes grown dim.
An old, old man!
Yet they bow with reverence low,
With respect they wait on him.

They gather at his side,
And in his way they throng:
Greet him with love and pride
The aged and the young.

And the children leave their play
As he passes on his way,
And afar off they follow
This old, old man.

He has gone down to the rock,
He is lying by the shore ;
He hath silent sate him down ;
And the young man, whose strong arm
Hath shielded him from harm,
Will not disturb the dream
That his spirit hovers o'er ;
And the gathered throng beside him
Group him on the shore.

Long he sits in silence,
The old, old man ;
While the waves with silvery reach
Go curling up the beach,
Or dash against the rocks in spray —
The huge rocks bedded deep
At the base of the proud steep,
Where the green ridge of Manomet
Grandly rises far away.

All the air is still,
And every distant hill
Its summit veils in soft, misty blue ;

Across the wide-spread bay,
Five-and-twenty miles away,
The white cliffs of Cape Cod hang in air,
As some mysterious hand,
Or enchanter's lifted wand,
Had suspended them, and charmed them there ;

And o'er all the waters wide,
And the hills in summer pride,
And the islands in the bay that rise,
And over Saquish Head
And the Gurnet's breakers dread,
The mild, soft sunlight like a blessing lies.

The old man's eyes grow bright
With the light of by-gone days ;
His voice is strong and clear,
His form no more is bowed,
He stands erect and proud,
And, dashing from his eye the indignant tear,
He turns him to the crowd that wait expectant
    near,
And reverent on him gaze ;
For they know that he has walked
In all the Pilgrim ways.

" Mark it well ! " he cries,
" Mark it well !
This rock on which we stand :
For here the honored feet
Of our fathers' exiled band
Pressed the land ;
And not the wide, wide world,
Not either hemisphere,
Has a spot in its domain
To freedom half so dear ! "
　　　　　　　— *Caroline Frances Orne.*

FIRST LANDING OF THE PILGRIMS.

DAYS pass, winds veer, and favoring skies
　　Change like the face of fortune ; storms
　　　　arise ;
Safely, but not within her port desired,
　　The good ship lies.
Where the long sandy cape
　　Bends and embraces round,
As with a lover's arm, the sheltered sea,
　　A haven she hath found
From adverse gales and boisterous billows free.

Now strike your sails,
Ye toil-worn mariners, and take your rest
Long as the fierce north-west
   In that wild fit prevails,
Tossing the waves uptorn with frantic sway.
   Keep ye within the bay,
   Contented to delay
Your course till the elemental madness cease,
And heaven and ocean are again at peace.

   How gladly there,
   Sick of the uncomfortable ocean,
The impatient passengers approach the shore ;
   Escaping from the sense of endless motion,
To feel firm earth beneath their feet once more,
   To breathe again the air
With taint of bilge and cordage undefiled,
And drink of living springs, if there they may,
And with fresh fruits and wholesome food repair
Their spirits, weary of the watery way.

   And oh ! How beautiful
   The things on earth appear
   To eyes that far and near
   For many a week have seen
Only the circle of the restless sea !

With what a fresh delight
They gaze again on fields and forests green,
　　Hovel, or whatsoe'er
May bear the trace of man's industrious hand!
　　How grateful to their sight
　　The shore of shelving sand,
As the light boat moves joyfully to land!

Woods they behold, and huts, and piles of wood,
　　And many a trace of toil,
But not green fields or pastures. 'T was a land
　　Of pines and sand ;
Dark pines that from the loose and sparkling soil
　　Rose in their strength aspiring : far and wide
　　They sent their searching roots on every side,
And thus, by depth and long extension, found
Firm hold and grasp within that treacherous
　　ground :
So had they risen and flourished, till the earth,
　　Unstable as its neighboring ocean there,
　　Like an unnatural mother, heaped around
Their trunks its wavy furrows white and high,
And stifled thus the living things it bore.
　　Half-buried thus they stand,
　　Their summits sere and dry,

Marking like monuments the funeral mound ;
As when the masts of some tall vessel show
Where, on the fatal shoals, the wreck lies
whelmed below.

—Robert Southey.

www.ingramcontent.com/pod-product-compliance
Lightning Source LLC
Chambersburg PA
CBHW030327270326
41926CB00010B/1536